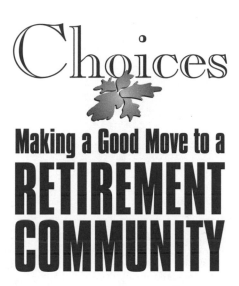

Choices

Making a Good Move to a
RETIREMENT
COMMUNITY

Heather M. Young PhD, ARNP • Rheba de Tornyay RN, EdD

Published by
ERA Care Communities
1325 Fourth Avenue, Suite 2110
Seattle, WA 98101 USA
Telephone: (206) 625-1515
Fax: (206) 625-9255
www.eracare.com

Young, Heather M.
Choices: Making a Good Move to a Retirement Community/Heather M. Young, Rheba de Tornyay.
Includes bibliographical references
ISBN 0-9710615-0-5
1.   Retirement communities, United States
2.   Aged Housing, United States
3.   Moving, Household, United States
4.   Life Change Events in Older Age, United States

Printed by Hignell Book Printing in Canada

A 1996 edition of this book was published by Slack, Incorporated, Thorofare, NJ.

Dedication

To Matthew Hosking Eddy, Heather's grandfather, whose vision in housing for the elderly and personal devotion to community service improved the lives of many older adults. His example and values are sources of great inspiration.

Contents

SECTION III: SETTLING IN

Chapter 7: Nesting

Chapter 8: Working Out Logistics

SECTION IV: SUCCESSFUL ADJUSTMENT

Chapter 9: Fitting In

APPENDICES

Acknowledgments

We thank Eli and Rebecca Almo for their strong commitment to honoring mothers and fathers, and their leadership in creating retirement communities to reflect that value.

The participants of this study deserve special recognition. We were profoundly moved by their experiences and are deeply grateful to them for their willingness to share their thoughts and lives with us. In particular, Luella Manus has had a special interest in seeing this book in print. Many residents of Ida Culver House Broadview in Seattle have also made contributions of content and encouragement.

This book is based on Heather Young's doctoral dissertation at the University of Washington School of Nursing, where Gail Wagnild, Sandra Eyres, Shirley Murphy and Michael Vitiello provided support, guidance and expertise throughout the research process.

Several people read and commented on the manuscript and we are grateful to them for their constructive advice and comments: Janet Beckmann, Hilke Faber, Helen Gregutt, Kristina Haight, Sue Hegyvary, Gail Powell-Cope, Patricia Stockdale and Jane Vaught.

Special thanks go to Ernlé and Margaret Young for their loving belief in their daughter and their willingness to provide both enthusiasm and critique.

We are grateful to the editorial staff at SLACK Incorporated. John Bond has provided wise counsel and guidance.

Finally, we express deep appreciation and love to our husbands, Peter Quinby and Rudy de Tornyay, for their friendship, support and understanding.

Introduction

If you are one of the 33 million Americans over the age of 65, this book is written with you in mind. You have survived the Great Depression and several wars. Like others who share a personal philosophy honed from early years of struggle against financial adversity, remaining independent is a major goal. Undoubtedly, you are concerned about your future, particularly when you read that one out of five people who reach age 65 to 70 will require the help of a caregiver. You may worry that you will be a burden to your children.

Four out of five seniors can make their own decisions and do just that. Many are enjoying freedom they never had before: free from the demands of work, family life, home maintenance, homemaking, free to pursue what is most enjoyable to them. With careful planning, they achieved their independence through analyzing what they want, what they need now and what they predict they may need later.

There is a growing trend for older people to live alone or in non-family settings. Thirty percent live alone; the majority are women. Yet older persons who live alone are a group at greater risk for eventual need for an institution, such as a nursing home, than those who live in a situation that can provide a network of support.

More people are seeking alternatives to nursing homes, such as retirement communities and assisted living complexes, that offer privacy and support to remain independent for as long as possible. Over four million older adults choose to live in retirement communities. You may have friends and family who have selected this option and you may be curious to find out if it's right for you.

Heather Young's doctoral dissertation explored the experience of moving into a retirement community for 21 adults who ranged in age from 72 to 96. Women made up almost three quarters of the group she studied. Rheba de Tornyay is an advocate of improved long-term care for an aging population. As registered nurses who work with older adults, both are interested in the process of adaptation to personal and environmental changes for people making the decision of where to live as they age.

We wanted to learn why it was that some people were better able to accommodate and assimilate change, while others felt defeated. To find out, we interviewed many people who made the decision to move into a retirement community. Most, but not all, were pleased with their decision. We became aware of the importance of a thread of continuity to maintain personal identity and integrity. We came to understand the importance of the echo of familiarity. We learned that often people needed information to sort out their options and make an informed decision. We believe that their stories may help you as you begin to cope with the complex issues you face.

The quotations in this book are real. We have eliminated or changed the names of the persons we interviewed to protect their privacy. The information provided came from many people, individually and in groups. We asked them what would have been helpful and supportive as they faced the thought of moving, and later as many made the decision to move into a retirement community. Finally, and we believe of greatest importance, we asked them what was involved in fitting in and adjusting to their new homes.

Through our work we have observed how others make the difficult but important decision about housing. Many told us that a stimulating environment improved the quality of their lives and presented positive, creative opportunities. Our interviews with people who have moved to retirement communities and other studies, give clear evidence that such a move can enhance the length of productive and meaningful years. Many shared the advice they would give others and said that they would have appreciated a guidebook as they were going through the process. Through sharing the words of others like you, we hope to help you understand what you need to consider in making the decision to move, what is involved in moving and the complex process of adjusting.

Of course, not all advice is suitable for everyone, but hearing some of their thoughts and ideas may be helpful to you in your thinking and planning. It may also raise questions that you may not have thought about yet.

Section I describes transitions and the changes you may experience as you contemplate your future. We hope to help you think through what your life is really like, and what your hopes are for the coming years. We suggest you begin your process with quiet contemplation and introspection.

Section II will help you plan and prepare for the move, if this is what you decide to do.

Section III is devoted to helping you settle in and find your place in a new environment, and offers practical suggestions to help you feel at home.

Section IV is about successful adjustment, including not only your personal adjustment but helping your children understand your new life.

Although we have written *Choices: Making A Good Move To A Retirement Community* primarily for readers who are thinking about or planning a move to a retirement community, we hope the book will be useful to those of you for whom this decision is not an immediate need. We learned from persons with whom we met and from other research studies that those who think and plan ahead make wiser decisions and are more satisfied with their choices. We hope this book will make a difference for you too. Whatever you decide to do, we offer our encouragement and best wishes.

Making the Decision

CHAPTER 1

Why Move?

The reasons for moving are as varied as the people who move. These are the stories of people who have very different reasons for thinking about moving to a retirement community: Mrs. Florence O'Brien, Mr. and Mrs. Leland Taylor and Miss Dorothy Lee.

Mrs. O'Brien became a widow 2 years ago and has lived in the same neighborhood for 45 years. She and her husband bought their home when their children were young and added on rooms as their family grew. She has a large garden with many lovely plants and shrubs. Her children have homes of their own and are busy with their families. In the past year, she has become more involved in social activities and volunteer work and finds that she is finally able to enjoy free time, after years of raising a family and managing a household. While she still loves her home and garden, she is finding it harder to manage the upkeep. Worry and guilt have replaced the joy she used to experience in nurturing her home. She is concerned that without the attention the house and yard need, the value of her home will decrease. Every time her taxes and utility bills go up, she wonders why she continues to pay for a large residence. Her needs have changed and she would rather have a more manageable home and the freedom to be as active as she chooses.

Mrs. O'Brien summarizes her thoughts in this way:

> My life has changed in the past few years—the kids had to move to another city, the house became a bigger chore to look after, my circle of friends grew a little smaller. I found that my needs and desires had changed. I began to realize that I had to start to make plans for where I would be in the future.

After carefully considering her options and what she felt she could afford, Mrs. O'Brien decided to move to a retirement community in her daughter's neighborhood.

Mr. and Mrs. Leland Taylor live in a two-story Tudor home, built 65 years ago. Mr. Taylor has developed severe arthritis in his hips and knees, resulting in difficulty getting around. He can no longer drive (Mrs. Taylor never learned to drive) and the cost and inconvenience of using taxis or buses for bringing home purchases from the grocery store or other shopping have become major concerns. They buy less when they go to the store, which affects their choice for meals. They do not like to rely on their daughter for transportation, and she is concerned that her parents are not able to manage their lives.

The Taylors find that their bathroom was not designed for people with limited mobility. Space to maneuver safely or comfortably is limited. It doesn't have safety bars to grab onto for help getting up from the toilet or getting into and out of the bathtub or shower. The stairs in their home are difficult for Mr. Taylor to manage. Mrs. Taylor worries about her husband if something should happen to her. Both are aware that their health is changing and want to make sure they can get the care they will need. The Taylor's decided to sign up for a meal program through the local senior center and modify their home to make it safer and more accessible, and have delayed making a decision to move.

Miss Lee worked downtown and has always lived in an attractive apartment near the city center. For many years she knew and enjoyed all her neighbors, but now most are strangers. She has become increasingly worried about her safety. Miss Lee just doesn't like the changes she has seen in her neighborhood; it doesn't feel the same anymore. She has started to stay home more because she doesn't want to venture out alone at night and is finding that her evenings have become lonely. She enjoys going to plays and being part of her church's choir and wishes she could continue with these meaningful outings.

This is what Miss Lee said:

When I first moved to this neighborhood, I knew everyone. I could talk to my neighbors and know they were interested in me and my welfare. Now I feel trapped in my own home. I won't go out after dark unless someone picks me up and delivers me to my door. I was always an outgoing person who enjoyed many activities. Now I'm depressed and feeling sorry for myself. I hate being constantly angry with my neighbors because they let their garden go, or they don't repair their porch. I hate seeing the neighborhood go to seed, and I can't wait for it to go completely downhill. So, I decided to move. It was the best decision I ever made.

Miss Lee moved to a retirement community near her previous home. As she states, she is very pleased with her move.

The experiences of these four people are typical of those who are thinking about moving, and highlight some common reasons why people start thinking about housing alternatives. If you are finding that your world is different or you are changing, it may be time to think about how to create the best situation for yourself while you have the energy and ability to make this important decision. If you are thinking about your housing needs for the future, you are not alone.

Living longer is only good if you can enjoy it. Maintaining control over your life as you age is central to that enjoyment, and where and with whom you live are important parts of retaining control. If you are at least 70 years old, it's time to think carefully about your living situation for the future. Statistics suggest that there is a good chance that most people will live a long life, so planning for it is a good idea. This means that you have to know what you need and want, and understand what you can afford financially before you begin exploring options. Planning for the major changes that might be part of your life as you age requires care, hard work and realistic thinking. The choices you ponder while you feel well are usually better and more thorough than the options available when you are under stress. If you make your decisions well ahead of a crisis while you are still healthy you can probably participate in the decisions rather than have someone else make them for you. The healthier you are, the easier, faster and better your adjustment will be to the changes you make.

Thinking about a future move provides an opportunity to make an active choice about the next years of your life and a chance to improve your circumstances. Moving may help you regain some control that may be slipping away. It may be that you are only beginning to think about leaving your home, or you may have made the decision already because you realize that you should move in the future. Either way, learning about your options will help you make a decision that is right for you. One housing solution doesn't fit everyone and with the tremendous range of personalities, preferences and needs of older adults, selecting a new home is not an easy task. What may have worked for friends or family may not be the best solution for you. You have to devote your own time and energy to select the best option because the decision to move is personal and will influence the quality of your life.

Moving as a Process

Moving is a process that takes place over time, starting with the first inclination of a future move, through the period of decision making, planning and coordinating the actual move and ending when the person feels settled and at home. A description of the process of moving will highlight the different phases of the move and help you make sense of this important event in your life. You will find that, contrary to the popular image of "moving" as that day when you transfer your possessions to a new location, moving is a series of events that may extend over a period of months to years. Interestingly, the chapter on the move itself is the shortest one in this book because the people we interviewed had less to say about it than the other events involved in the move. An understanding of the moving process can help you anticipate changes, get the resources and support you need and make the entire transition more comfortable.

Research has confirmed what most of us know intuitively: People who participate in making important life decisions tend to be happier with the outcomes of those decisions. In particular, older adults who play a major role in selecting their new home and planning the move are generally more satisfied and adjust more readily. No matter how much another person has your welfare at heart and how helpful he or she is in your decision-making process, it is best if you make this important decision for yourself.

What Are My Choices?

There are many considerations in choosing housing and several possibilities. While we briefly highlight a few other options, the

---

major focus of this book is on retirement communities because this is an increasingly common choice among older adults, and it is also the setting for our research and practice.

In considering your options, you will need to reflect on your lifestyle, your financial circumstances, your own health and that of your spouse. There are some choices that allow you to remain in your current home; some mean moving to a relative's home or near it. If you stay in your current home or move to a relative's home, this may involve physical modification of the residence. Many communities offer supportive services for persons needing help in meeting daily needs who wish to remain in their current home.

If you wish to remain in your home and the major reason you are considering a move is limited finances, be aware that there are housing assistance programs for low income older adults that could help you stay at home. Help with utility expenses through home energy inspections and lowered rates, and reduction in property taxes or rent are two examples of the assistance offered to eligible seniors in many communities.

For some persons, moving to a smaller home or to a condominium may prolong their years of independence. A great deal depends on the true reason for making the move. Some people who eventually move into a retirement community feel that the transition was smoother for them because they had experienced the interim step of being in smaller living quarters. They had pared down their possessions and adjusted to a new living situation before making the decision to join a retirement community. Others wanted to make only one move, and they appreciated the chance to grow accustomed to the community, take advantage of the programs offered and establish friendships before their health and abilities declined and they needed more help.

Other housing alternatives include building or moving to an accessory apartment, an area built into or onto an existing house. This allows you to live independently without being alone completely. Another option is the Elder Cottage Housing Opportunity, called ECHO housing. These are small, self-contained, manufactured units that can be placed, if city zoning allows, in the yard of a single family house to allow elders to live near their families while retaining privacy and independence. Both options require a thorough knowledge of housing regulations in local communities.

Sharing a home with others, including adult children, is an option that appeals to some people. However, living successfully with your adult children requires careful consideration by all concerned. Think realistically and honestly about how such a living situation would affect your well-being and that of your child and your child's family. You will need to consider how each member of the household would contribute and how you would manage the potential challenges of a multigenerational family.

Retirement communities are relatively new in our society. There are a variety of housing choices within the general umbrella of "retirement" or "congregate" housing. Making sense of these options can be complex and often confusing. Even the definitions are unclear because they include various combinations of services and financial arrangements. It is impossible to tell what a community provides strictly from either its name or its label.

A retirement community provides a residential atmosphere where you have your own private apartment of varying size. Although you may share some of your meals in a central dining room, there usually is a compact kitchen in which you can prepare some of your meals. These facilities often offer some housekeeping services, and commonly there are staff available to organize social and recreational activities. There may be transportation for group activities and you probably can arrange some for private appointments, like going to the doctor. A retirement community differs from fully independent living, such as an apartment or a condominium, because of the services and staff available to provide for your safety, physical well-being and companionship.

Amenities, such as a swimming pool, hobby rooms, spaces for gardening and even tennis courts or a golf course, vary a great deal among the communities. Some retirement communities offer extra services for an added fee, such as additional meals or assistance with activities of daily living (dressing, getting to meals and personal hygiene). Some have the capacity for medication supervision and other nursing services. These are licensed as "Boarding Homes" or "Assisted Living Facilities" because they provide personal care and protective oversight as needed. The more amenities, space and service a community offers, the higher the price.

In shopping for a housing community, it is essential to make sure you are comparing apples to apples, not apples to oranges.

Communities package their programs and services in different ways, with some providing a general package that is available for a standard cost to everyone. Others separate the various charges and fees and offer more flexibility in selecting the services and programs. In Appendix D we provide a checklist for shopping and comparing communities.

Financial Arrangements

There are two major types of financial arrangements for retirement communities. One is a rental contract in which you sign a lease for a set time giving you the right to live in the apartment and receive specified services for a monthly fee. You may cancel the lease when the agreed upon time ends. The facility may be able to provide added services for additional fees. It is important that you know in advance what services are included, and also what is available for an added charge. As a rule, rental agreements do not include health care services for a prolonged period of time.

If your financial resources are limited, housing subsidized by the government for older adults is available in many communities. To find out about it, contact your local housing authority, or the local Area Agency on Aging.

The other financial arrangement is called a "life use fee." This is commonly seen in continuing care retirement communities (CCRCs) that offer a full range of housing, residential services and health care to older residents as their needs change. All CCRCs have financial requirements for entry into the community and require some degree of financial disclosure to assess your ability to meet their financial obligations. Because a CCRC involves a substantial financial commitment on your part, we strongly suggest that if you are considering this type of retirement community you seek further counsel from your financial advisor. CCRCs also assess the health of those applying to the community and some exclude certain pre-existing medical conditions from their coverage. Most require residents to carry Medicare Parts A and B, and some require coverage by supplemental and long-term care insurance.

You may worry about what would happen to you if you fell seriously ill. Or, if you died, what would happen to your spouse? The CCRC consists of housing where residents live independently and receive certain residential services such as meals, activities, housekeeping and maintenance. Support services for disabled residents who require assistance with activities of daily living are offered. The major difference is that health care services for those who become temporarily ill or require long-term care are included in the contract. With the exception of hospital admission, health care is provided on site. There are many types of CCRC agreements and they differ in two major ways: the amount of health care that is included in the agreement, and how you pay for the accommodations, services and health with entry and monthly fees. Extensive agreements guarantee skilled nursing care, modified agreements limit the amount of guaranteed care, and fee-for-service agreements enable residents to pay for care as it is needed, usually for a lower entry fee.

Based on the principle of self-insurance, every continuing care arrangement involves a contract between residents and the CCRC that, at a minimum, guarantees shelter and access to various health care services for the balance of the resident's lifetime. In return, the resident agrees to pay a lump-sum entrance fee when moving to the community and monthly payments after that. Most CCRC contracts contain a clause governing refund of the entrance fee if the contract is ended by the resident and/or the resident dies. Depending on the contract, entrance fees may be nonrefundable, refundable on a decreasing basis over time, partially refundable or fully refundable.

It is essential that you understand your contract before signing. It is also important that both your legal and financial advisors review your contract prior to your agreement. There are many excellent CCRCs that offer you the security you seek, but there have been instances where particular CCRCs have not been financially solvent, and when they folded, their residents lost their equity. As people are living longer, some CCRCs did not plan for the increased longevity and are unable to continue to meet the long-term care needs of their residents. If you are interested in learning more about CCRCs it will be helpful to write for *The Consumer's Directory to Continuing Care Retirement Communities*, listed in Appendix E. It details the available options and has cost comparison worksheets that you may find helpful. Each accredited community profile is listed by state and contains addresses with a description of the setting, style of community, sponsor and fee information.

Where Do I Start?

It is beyond the scope of this book to go into detail about all housing alternatives, so we present a method for investigating the options available so that you may make a well-informed decision. We will focus on retirement living and the process of deciding, moving and adjusting that may help you in thinking about relocation, no matter what type of housing you seek.

Because you are unique, it is impossible for anyone to tell you what is best for you. However, if you are like most of the people we interviewed, you may not be certain about what you want yourself. Many people who start to explore retirement housing begin with only a vague idea of what they are seeking. Although you have adjusted to previous moves, you may worry whether you will be happy making a major change at this stage in your life. It isn't easy to think of selling your home, and deciding what possessions to keep and what to give away. It isn't easy to decide whether you want to rent or buy into a retirement community. The very thought of making the move itself and sorting through your closets, attic and basement may concern you so much that you put off thinking about it. Your children may be pressuring you to sell, or they may be so upset at the thought of your leaving the home in which they spent many years that you can't face the prospect of even discussing it with them.

If you do not have, or if you have lost, a life partner, you should know the advantages of being near other people. There is evidence, based on research findings, that living alone can be a significant health risk. It is difficult to prepare and eat a balanced diet when you live alone. Loneliness and boredom are the enemies of good mental health. If an accident or illness occurs while you are home alone, the consequences may be more severe than with quick detection and treatment. These are important considerations to keep in mind as you think about your future housing.

We hope that the experiences of others will enable you to make sense of these many considerations. The approach we use is one that helps you think about your lifestyle, what you want now and what you may need in the future. We will suggest ways to go about looking for and evaluating retirement communities. We will also discuss the adjustment process to help you understand some phases you will face if you move. There is no perfect answer for everyone, but it is important that you keep in mind that you have choices. It is also important that you emphasize what you will be gaining from your move, not what you think you will miss from your current life.

We suggest that you first read through the entire book. Although not all parts will be important to you at all stages in your deliberations, it should be helpful to know what the book can offer you. Take the self-tests as a guide in your thinking. You may want to copy the tests so that you can use them later if your needs change.

CHAPTER 2

Understanding Transitions

In this chapter we ask you to take the time to be introspective about your life, your previous major life changes, who you are and what you are becoming. These are thoughts and discussions that you need to have for yourself and probably by yourself. If you have a life partner, each of you needs to think separately, and then you may want to discuss your lives together.

Understanding Transitions as Experiences

Throughout life we experience transitions, such as changes in our relationships and marital status, parenting, grandparenting and changes in role. Education and working can trigger transitions. As we age, we face the transition of becoming an adult, then the changes in life as we become older. Each time a major life event occurs, our personal identities change, evolve and develop. Psychologists describe development as a series of life changes and transition points.

William Bridges, a consultant in human development, talks about the three stages of transitions. The first is the ending of a previous situation. It is a period of disruption in which assumptions about the world are questioned and former ways of relating are not consistent with current circumstances. Endings may be times of great joy or sadness as we bid farewell to people or circumstances. He calls the second phase the neutral zone. This is a period of feeling disconnected and empty, and it is characterized by a diffuse sense of identity. During this time old ways of doing things are no longer adequate, but we have yet to figure out new ways of thinking and behaving. The neutral zone may be a period of solitude and tremendous inner growth. The final stage, the new beginning, emerges as the reawakening period. It is during this last phase that mobilization of new resources and the creation of different purpose and meaning occurs. Life starts to seem normal again, and there is a re-establishment of routines and relationships. So, remember that a new beginning follows an ending—a pattern that represents the way we change and grow. Bridges also points out that although most people really do not want to think about larger issues while they are in the turmoil of transition, it is important to deal with these issues to understand not only what is happening, but why.

Moving can be an important life transition with the goal of not only feeling settled in your new home but finding new meaning in your life. It is helpful to think of it as having several phases. Change is a part of moving, not just a change in your physical environment, but also in your social contacts, feelings about yourself, your circumstances and your daily routine. The decision to move represents certain endings. It includes, perhaps, goodbyes to long-time neighbors, leaving familiar surroundings, such as stores where you shop, routes you walk and people whom you meet daily. You must part with some of your furniture and other things you have collected. Your future may seem uncertain and unsettled. As you progress through the phases of moving your plans become clearer, and as you complete your move, you will find a return to your sense of security. A feeling of being at home again heralds your new beginning and a sense of being settled. Typically, people who move find that it takes several months to complete the transition and feel at home in their new residence.

Moving as Development

Think of moving as a part of life development. Throughout life, we face challenges that force us to "move" in some way or another, whether by a physical change or a move in the way we look at a situation. We all connect with people and circumstances and then have to part from them later in life. Think of it as an opportunity to grow in self-awareness and abilities.

It might be helpful to look back over your own development. As events and stages in your life required change, you incorporated these situations into your life and developed a new meaning and understanding. For example, a school age child has to grapple with leaving his or her family and becoming part of a new peer group.

Persons who retire from a job they enjoyed have to separate from the work world and seek new involvement in social relationships and meaningful activities. At each change there is a tension between what was and what will be. There is also an opportunity to revisit old developmental issues at a new level of maturity and complexity. There is research suggesting that searching for meaning through a major life change is a stimulus for personal growth and development.

A major reason we suggest that you take the time and effort to think of your experiences is so that you may appreciate the complexity of life changes you have already undergone and those you may anticipate with moving. The creative efforts over time to establish a new home, make new friends and find your place in the new community take energy and appreciation of your past.

Mrs. Jacobs is a retired secretary who lost her husband two years before she made the decision to move to a retirement community.

Following are her words:

> I had a terrible time making the decision to move. I always thought of myself in terms of both my job and being a wife and mother. I rattled around my home looking for things to do and family to take care of. It was very distressing to me and I kept wanting to go back to who I used to be. Then one day I woke up and realized that the past was gone, and that I had better say goodbye to it all and move on. Having made that decision, I went through several weeks being neither the person I was nor the person I was to become. It was very disorienting to me. My

family thought I was ill, but I really wanted to be by myself for a while. Then after I made the decision I was so busy I didn't have time to worry. I was able to get going again.

Important Factors in Adjustment

Relocation is a transition that happens in the context of other major changes in your life. You may be contemplating your move in association with alterations in health, financial status or social network of support. You are undoubtedly asking the important question: How do I know if I can adjust to the major change in my life of moving to a retirement community? It should be helpful to hear what others who have made a successful adjustment have to say.

One characteristic most associated with successful adjustment is resilience. Resilience is the ability to adapt successfully despite risk and adversity. It is the ability to be flexible in the face of change. Resilient people have five major qualities.

- They are self-reliant, meaning that they believe in themselves and in their own abilities.

- They persevere and continue to try something even if they feel discouraged.

- They have equanimity and peace of mind to maintain balance and take the ups and downs of life in stride.

- Life has meaning for them and they value their contributions.

- Finally, they recognize that while they share many of their experiences with others, there are some things in life that must be faced alone.

Resilient people make the most of their lives and emphasize positive things while minimizing the negative. Research shows that those who are less resilient have more difficulty with change and may not be as successful with a major move.

In describing the characteristics of resilience, this is what others have said. These are the words of a woman reflecting on self-reliance:

> I think I can rise to a situation regardless of what it is. I've had to all the way through. I think that if you can live through something it makes you a little stronger for anything more that comes.

Every person over the age of 60 knows the value of hard work and personal sacrifice. This important characteristic associated with resilience is perseverance. This is the strength of not giving up, even if the situation doesn't look hopeful. These are people who have the philosophy of living one day at a time. One woman had this to say after a series of catastrophic events in her life:

> You have to figure you're going to have to keep going regardless, that's all. You got to get going in the right direction. You know it's not going to be of any help if we get too far down. I think we'll stay here and then we'll work up. We're getting there.

Another characteristic of resilience is equanimity, or the ability to see life within a broader perspective. The phrase "roll with the punches" describes it. We all have ups and downs, and experience has taught us that an up follows a down. A woman recognized that she couldn't dwell in the past as she said this:

> You can't worry about the past now, it's gone. You can't brood over something you can't do anything about. If you lose something, you lose something. That's the only way to look at it in my estimation, because you have to take life as it comes and goes. We had lots of ups and downs, but I guess everybody does. You have to learn to laugh and keep a balance.

Meaningfulness is the ability to remain engaged and active and place value in what you do. The presence of faith and hope enhances a sense of meaning. For many, faith in God and religion are important sources of meaning; other people view faith as spirituality. Keeping busy is an active approach to creating meaning. Finding ways to remain active is important, as this woman said:

> You know, the more you look at the needs of others, you realize that time can be spent in such a pleasant way, helping other people. It gives your life great meaning.

Being able to face life by yourself is an important factor in resilience. As the social network of friends diminishes in later life, this ability to accept your solitude is essential.

This man said it well:

> I can get along with myself and I don't need a lot of fol-
> lowers. I don't have to depend on a lot of other people. As
> long as you are on top you've got lots of friends, and
> when you get down here you've got none. So I don't build
> a friendship that I can't get along without.

How Do I Know If I Will Adjust?

You know yourself and how you have coped with past change.
To help you further, take the Resilience Test in Appendix A. This
short set of questions will help you assess your resilience.

What Has Been My Previous Experience in Moving?

Another important predictive factor in how you will adjust to a
move is your previous experience with moving. Think of all of your
previous moves and what you have learned from them. Remember
how you felt and what you feared, from small things to larger
aspects. Most moves made in early life take place in response to
opportunities—a new job or pursuing education. Even moves made
for positive reasons entail certain choices and sacrifices.

Depending on your circumstances, you may not feel that you
really want this move. In contrast to previous moves, you may find
yourself lower on energy and enthusiasm about the change. Think
about your previous experiences with moving—what made the

move successful? What would you do differently? How did you make your new house a home? How did you cope with the sacrifices you made by moving? By reflecting on your own experience, you can probably identify strategies that will make this move the best it can be.

It is helpful to turn again to research findings to help understand the effects of moving to a retirement community. Compared to tenants relocating to traditional housing (smaller houses, apartments, condominiums) those moving to retirement communities show greater increases in morale and well-being, improved housing satisfaction and a larger social network. It is also important to realize that in these studies residents in retirement communities lessened their activities outside their retirement communities, choosing to limit their major involvements to the social and service provisions of their new home. This may be an important point to keep in mind as you seek a community in which to live.

To summarize the possible personal effects of your move, remember again that for each person the circumstances leading to the move, the meaning associated with the changes and the subsequent events and responses are unique. In the next chapter we will give practical advice for deciding whether to move.

CHAPTER 3

Deciding Whether to Move

In the first chapter we identified some common reasons people think of making a move to a retirement community. There are many reasons for moving from a home to a shared living environment. We present what others have said about why they decided to make the move to stimulate thoughts about your situation. In this chapter we will help you identify why you may want to move, and specifically what you think you need.

Reasons for Moving

A variety of circumstances prompt thinking about moving, including home maintenance, transportation, life changes, safety and security. A major reason for wanting to move is that the tasks of maintaining a large home and yard become overwhelming, particularly when the household becomes smaller and the demands of caring for the premises continue to increase. This is what one woman had to say:

> I was married to a Mr. "Fix-it", and he did everything. I took care of the books, and he took care of fixing-it. My glory, he died, and things started to break down. There I was, I had to get a man to mow the lawn, I had to get a man to cut the trees. And then, you know, in a house that you've lived in for 23 years, things broke down when he wasn't there to keep them going. I was having quite a time getting things together.

The costs and coordination of household services and repairs may be burdensome. Older homes begin to have more maintenance needs and the expense and difficulty of obtaining reliable repairs may be troublesome. Homeowners worry that their property will decrease in value if they are not able to maintain their standards of home repair and appearance.

Getting around the neighborhood can pose unique problems, particularly if you don't drive. If public transportation is available for you to use, it may be inconvenient or you could be afraid to use it depending on your neighborhood. Managing grocery shopping is more difficult without a private car to bring the purchases home. A common change with age is difficulty with night driving, resulting in reluctance to go out after dark. When you don't feel you can drive easily, you can't shop, participate in important social activities or see your friends. In the words of another woman:

> Without the car I had no way of getting groceries and all those things, so we used a taxi quite a bit, and depended

on our kids, but you hate to do that. I had to have some-body deliver the milk and I had to have somebody help to get to the store and back, and ah, it's just silly, so we decided the best thing to do was to sell.

Sometimes a major event leaves little choice in the decision to move. One couple had a fire and as a result they began thinking about whether they should rebuild or move. This is what they said:

I figure we hadn't had the fire we'd still be in the house. That prompted everything, that started the ball rolling. Then you get so far down, you might as well make up your mind and go someplace else. But you know, there always has to be an initial start, to change your lifestyle. Otherwise you'd just stay there.

Many life experiences can contribute to the decision to make a move. Your health may be changing or you worry about what you would do if you faced a health emergency. The death of a spouse or significant other may lead to a change of home with the opportunity to meet new people. In the words of a woman:

My son felt that I should not live alone in the house and he felt that living in a group arrangement like this with people would be what I needed. I don't know how much the doctor contributed to that. On the other hand, I have a friend and her daughter doesn't want her to leave her home, and she doesn't want to, and she's not with people nearly as much as I am, even when I was in my home.

Safety and security often motivate a move, particularly when the crime rate in the neighborhood increases. If you feel more vulnerable or become aware of threats to your security, the need to survive can dominate your life, with little energy or enthusiasm left for pleasurable activities. Another woman had this to say:

> I truly never thought I'd leave this house. I lived here since the early years of my marriage and I raised my three kids here. But the neighborhood has changed and when I learned that someone had been attacked in his own home, just four blocks from here, it was really a sobering thought. I'm alone now — what would I do if I answered the bell and there stood a person with a mask over his head? I shudder about it and I just can't get it out of my mind. So, I decided it was better to move now and stop worrying than stay here, as much as I hated to leave.

For most people we interviewed, the reason for moving to a retirement community was different from the reasons given for their former moves. They all recognized, or were encouraged to do this by their families, that living totally independently was no longer desirable and that they needed relief from the chores associated with meal preparation and housework. They also gave companionship and the support of others nearby as reasons for moving. This is different from previous moves that were more commonly made in response to opportunities—a job promotion, the chance to pursue more education, moving to a larger home as the family grew.

It is important for you to keep in mind that a move brings potential for positive benefit. Many people who move to a retirement community say that they wish they had made the decision earlier. They cite the relief from managing a household, the luxury of having someone else worry about cooking, the varied social events, new friendships and the knowledge that there are others near if you need them as the most compelling reasons to move. Often events have both negative and positive effects—even the most desired choices involve some sacrifice or compromise.

Staying in Your Own Home

There are many considerations in deciding to stay in your own home, including how to manage the activities of daily life. Most older people express a general desire to stay in their home as long as possible. This can involve considerable planning and commitment by friends and family members, once you are unable to manage the demands of living completely independently. If you are weighing your options and considering staying where you are, think about how you manage now and how you would manage should you become unable to drive, shop, get to appointments, manage your finances, complete your daily hygiene activities or communicate with others. If you live near family members or friends who are willing and able to provide additional assistance, your chances of continued success in your own home are greater. It may seem paradoxical, but the decision to move to a retirement community can actually be an act of independence, in that you are choosing a setting that can provide necessary support instead of relying on the assistance of your family and friends.

EXERCISE:
> Take a few moments to list your strongest reasons for staying in your current home. Then list the strongest reasons you can think of for moving to another setting.

Consider the location of your home in relation to the services and people you want to be near, the physical characteristics of your home and neighborhood, any recent problems or concerns you have had in your home, any anticipated events or changes and your feelings about moving. If you can identify at least a couple of reasons to move to another setting, it is worth continuing with your exploration of this decision.

As you read the following chapters, keep in mind the reasons you might want to move and what is important to you. The better you understand your needs, the better your choice will be and the longer you can take advantage of a particular living situation.

Who Will Make the Decision?

How you make the decision to move will usually follow the way you have made significant choices in the past. It is worthwhile to reflect on your own decision-making patterns and the influences you consider when you make important choices. Do you typically make decisions by gathering all the facts yourself and analyzing your options, or do you tend to be more spontaneous or instinctive? When you face a dilemma, who do you usually consult—your spouse, your friends, your children or no one? At what point do you like to seek the opinions of others—early in the process or after you have made a preliminary decision?

Although there is no one right way to make an important decision that has consequences for your future satisfaction, research suggests that people who are not involved in some part of the process have the most difficulty with their future adjustment. Even when circumstances speed up the decision process and of may preclude active participation in the entire selection, it is important for you to be a part of the final choice. Deciding to move can be an opportunity to maintain control over your circumstances and of your destiny. No matter how involved your family may be, you can actively establish new future roles for yourself and for your family. If you can state your needs clearly and share your feelings about the kind of support and freedom you are seeking, you can also remove guilt and concern from those who love you, and can shape the role that they will play. In Chapter 10, we will focus specifically on dealing with family members throughout the moving process.

How Far Ahead Do I Want to Plan?

There are two main approaches to planning—you can wait until you need the services of a retirement community environment, or you can plan and make the move early. Those who wait until they think they really need a retirement community environment often miscalculate and find that their needs exceed the limits of independent living. Those who plan and make a move when they are healthy and energetic find that they can take full advantage of the social, recreational and service programs. They can become settled and make friends and enjoy the benefits of a communal setting. Planning for a move does not mean that you have to make the move right away, but thinking about your values, your needs and your potential options in advance will make the process easier when you do decide to do this.

If you are beginning to think about your future you have taken the most important first step. The best time to explore your options is before a crisis arises. Many people describe their move to retirement communities as their last *chosen* move, in that an emergency did not force the move, and they had the opportunity to participate to the fullest extent in the decision and experience. Planning helps to take the emotional reaction out of difficult decisions and allows you to be objective.

Interestingly, if you are like most people, you have planned for your death better than for your life. Many older people, whatever their finances, have some form of will in place stating how they want to distribute their possessions. Some even have purchased burial plots and paid for their funeral in advance. But planning for where and how you want to live comfortably and safely may be harder to accomplish.

What Is My Financial Outlook?

How much do you feel you can comfortably pay for rent and other personal services now? Are you prepared for the increasing cost of living? Or do you want to buy into a continuing care facility so you don't have to worry about planning for your future health needs? You need to consider the value of your current assets, your monthly income, any expected changes in assets or income and your expenses. It is helpful to list all your assets (the value of your home and investments), and your sources of income (including social security, retirement pensions, interest and notes due to you). Then you should list all your current expenses (mortgage or rent, property taxes, utilities, services, health care, food, entertainment, transportation, etc.).

When considering moving into a retirement community, make an accurate comparison with your current situation and seek the advice of a financial professional. Appendix B offers a worksheet to guide your assessment of costs. When evaluating the proposed rental rate, identify what that fee includes, for example, rent, food, housekeeping, transportation and other services. Compare this figure to your current costs for all of those items, not just your mortgage payment. For example, if meals are included in the rental rate, consider your monthly food expenses (cost of groceries, transportation and preparation of meals) so that you may make a more meaningful comparison with your current monthly housing expense.

It is difficult to know what your future financial needs will be, as your longevity, health and functional ability will influence your expenses. One couple discussed the financial situation they faced:

> We're just fine if we don't live more than 5 or 6 years longer. We won't have any problems. But beyond that we don't know. And if inflation continues, that might make a difference. We don't have much income anymore. A very small amount of investments, not enough to get excited about, but it's there. We worked awfully hard for our money.

Unless you have long-term care insurance, you must pay out of pocket for most independent or assisted living programs. Under the current health care system, Medicare Part A may pay for a limited time in a long-term care facility as you recuperate from being in the hospital and meet eligibility requirements. Medicaid funds skilled nursing care, assisted living and home services for people who are medically eligible and have exhausted the ability to pay privately, meeting financial criteria. As available programs and eligibility criteria vary state by state, you should contact your local Area Agency on Aging for further information about government-sponsored programs.

As you plan, you might consider what you would like to pay per month for housing and what your limits would be. If you have a home to sell, the money you receive may be invested to give you a source of monthly income. This is important as you explore your options and add up the costs of different facilities. The worksheets we provide in Appendix B are for your guidance only. It is exceedingly important that you consult both your financial and tax adviser for help in this important decision.

What Is My Health Outlook?

How long you can live independently depends on your ability to manage your basic activities of daily living, such as bathing, dressing, eating and toileting. Other activities such as shopping, preparing meals and balancing the checkbook are also factors. If you are having difficulty with any of these activities now, there is a chance that you will be in need of some personal care assistance in the future. It will be more crucial to think of a facility that offers help with these activities.

You may have already lost your life partner and it is now time to readjust your life to that of being a single person. Or you and your spouse may be fortunate to still have each other and you want to make your plans together. If so, both your own health and that of your spouse are important considerations. How healthy are you now? How long did your parents live? Do you or your spouse have any chronic health problems that may require additional assistance? Consider how frequently you see your health care provider currently—is it important to stay close by because of your relationship with your provider or your health plan? Certain chronic illnesses, such as Parkinson's disease, heart disease or cancer require ongoing monitoring. If this is an important aspect of your care, think about how you would get to your provider and who you would call in an emergency. These considerations could influence the location you select.

What Are My Next Steps?

Now that you have completed the important first step of identifying your needs, figuring out your financial status and considering your health status, it is time to begin thinking of what you want and need in a housing facility. You may consider where your friends and family live and your desired geographical location. Do you want to go where the sun shines more?

What is your lifestyle? Do you like to play golf or bridge, swim, go to the theater or shop? It is important that you know your preferences and what factors to consider as you make your plans. Chapter 4 will help you find out the answers to these and other questions.

Deciding Where to Move

In this chapter we will help you identify what you are looking for to satisfy your needs and whether retirement housing is an acceptable choice. You will need to think about your preferences and interests—what brings you the most pleasure and what aspects you would like to change in your current living situation. Is location a significant factor? What type of neighborhood do you prefer? What style of community do you want? What services are important to you? Is being near family and friends essential? Only you can figure out the critical features of your new home.

As we described in the first chapter, a retirement community provides a residential environment with shared common space, such as a dining room, lobby, recreational space or other amenities. Residents live independently in their own apartments with some services provided, such as meals, housekeeping, recreational activities and transportation. Many communities also have an assisted living facility. This is designed for people who need personal care, for example, help with dressing, grooming, bathing or medication supervision. There is an additional fee for personal care services, based on individual needs. As you evaluate your needs and expectations, you may think about whether retirement communities offer the services and amenities that you're seeking. Some retirement communities and all CCRCs also include a skilled nursing facility, providing the services of registered nurses, physical and occupational therapists and other health care professionals.

Community Characteristics

Relocation is complex and multifaceted. The first step in making the critical decision of where you may live the rest of your life is deciding what is important to you. Having an organized method of thinking through your values is the key to choosing a community with the characteristics you prefer. Take the self-test in Appendix C to help you find out if a retirement community is right for you.

It is unrealistic to expect that moving to a new setting will recreate a home exactly like the one you have now. You can, however, ensure that you find the crucial aspects of what you consider home in your new dwelling. List the essential elements in a living situation and include physical features. The approximate size of the community may be significant. Do you prefer a small, more intimate community of less than 25 units, or a large community of over 100 units?

Some people want to be part of a large community because they love variety and they enjoy the relative anonymity of being surrounded by many people; others prefer what they perceive to be the warmth of a smaller, more intimate group. A larger community can offer more recreational activities because larger groups of residents share the costs.

Have you given thought to the style of the community, such as a high-rise, mid-rise or sprawling campus-type residential community? Are you most comfortable in a modest community that is not lavish, or do you like and can you afford a luxury unit with large apartments and elegant dining rooms? What services are likely to be essential to you in the future? Do you want to live near family and friends? Do you want to be with people who are like you in their ethnic, religious or educational backgrounds? Do you like an urban setting with shopping, recreation and health services within walking distance? Do you prefer a suburban, small town or rural setting if transportation is available? Would you prefer a swimming pool? Would a nearby tennis court or golf course be an added incentive? These and other lifestyle considerations may influence your choice.

The location is probably the first issue to settle, deciding upon the desired city, town or neighborhood. Many people choose a community based on their current neighborhood or that of their family members. Staying in your neighborhood promotes continuity, as you'll be able to shop in the same stores, visit old friends and continue many of your current routines. Some neighborhoods, however, are not ideal for older adults and a move to a new neighborhood may open many new opportunities. Factors such as proximity to shopping, banking and health care are worth your consideration.

Some people choose a retirement location in a place where they can enjoy recreational and leisure activities. For these people, a golf course, swimming pool, hiking trails and other active lifestyle amenities are important factors. If you want to build your entire life around recreational activities and socialize frequently, then a retirement community focused on recreation is ideal. A number of these communities are located in Florida, Arizona and California.

Although a life filled with play and recreation may have been your dream when you were younger and earning a living, recreation alone may not satisfy you enough to form the basis for your decisions at this stage in your life. You may want to spend your time learning and growing. The development of specialized adult communities that focus on lifelong learning in locations near colleges and universities is an emerging trend in retirement communities. Even if you choose a location some distance from an educational institution, ask about the community's offerings to find out if educational courses, lectures and transportation to intellectual activities are an active part of the community's programming. Proximity to a library could also be important to you; access to computer technology could open many other opportunities.

If you choose a community composed of active, intellectually stimulating residents, you will enhance the chance of finding travel companions to enjoy new experiences. The tremendous success of Elderhostel, a self-supporting, nonprofit program that combines travel, learning and leisure for older adults attests to the need for the excitement of continuing to learn.

A major myth about aging is that older people have nothing more to contribute to society. Studies have repeatedly shown that as people grow older, they have a marked tendency to become more interested in giving more to others than they receive. If volunteering is important to you, find out what exists near the location you are considering. If you want to help children, proximity to a school or playground may be important. If you want to help those who are ill, then being near a hospital, nursing home or other health facility may be necessary. Figure out for yourself what gives you satisfaction, and then be certain that these activities exist in your targeted area.

Features of the service package may influence your decision; for example, the service and financial arrangements for meals and housekeeping. Other characteristics you may want to consider are costs, who lives there and the general culture of the environment. If you have specific requirements, such as keeping pets or preferring a church-run organization, include these in your list as well. Take your time and list all the things that are important to you.

After you have compiled the list of essentials, consider other aspects that may influence your decision. Does a flexible meal plan appeal to you, instead of paying for all your meals as part of your monthly rent? As you think about a typical day and the kinds of interests you have, what will you need in a living environment to continue to find meaning and enjoyment?

Shopping for a Retirement Community

Now you need to evaluate your options. Based on the values and needs you have identified, your next step is to visit the communities in your chosen geographic area. Prepare a list of items you most want to learn about. To help you compare the communities you visit, a checklist is provided in Appendix D. Remember that communities may package their services differently and it is important to know what the base fee covers and what services are offered at an additional cost.

To find out what exists in your local area, call the Senior Information and Assistance hotline in your community. The number can be found in the telephone book under State Government and, you may also check the public library and the Yellow Pages of the telephone directory where retirement communities advertise. We recommend that you call several communities and request information and brochures.

Once you have gathered current information, you may narrow your search to a few communities that are of particular interest to you. At this point it is useful to plan visits to your leading choices. Even if you identify one community that seems far more desirable than others, still plan to visit a few so that you can compare. When you visit any community, be sure that you talk to both staff and residents. Many communities encourage people who are interested in living there to attend some community activities or meals. It is helpful to taste the food and spend time observing community life to see if it appeals to you. Talk to some of the residents to find out whether you would like to live with them. Recommendations of friends or acquaintances who live in retirement communities are very helpful. People who have experience can provide an insider's view of the features of a particular setting. Ask for copies of newsletters, menus, activity calendars and other literature about the community.

Achieving a Satisfactory Fit

After you have carefully looked at your needs and values and have a sense of the options that are available to you, it's time to put the two together and think about the best fit between your particular needs and the features of the retirement community settings you have explored. Remember that people vary in their priorities and needs, just as communities vary in their amenities and services. The most crucial consideration is how a particular community fits with your unique needs. This is what a woman said:

> I visited about six retirement homes and each was different. I finally found one that just seemed to feel right. I don't know how to explain it. I had lunch there and the people seemed friendly and like me. I even found a woman I used to work with and she was so enthusiastic, I felt I had come home. I don't drive anymore, and this place is right nearby to the mall and they have a bus that takes us places — it's ideal for me. My advice to others is to visit many communities until you find it feels right.

And now read what a man said:

> My wife was failing and I realized that we had to move,
> but I just didn't know where to go or how to begin. So our
> daughter found out where the retirement communities
> were and we went visiting to a few. I guess we made the
> decision too quickly, because although I liked the looks
> of the place, I don't feel at home with the people. They
> just aren't friendly. I wish we had gone to a home where
> people of our religion were. I feel like a stranger here.

Moving: Loss and Opportunity

Moving and experiencing a new lifestyle, as with all major life
decisions, presents a complex mixture of potential benefits and possible sacrifices. Think back on other moves you have made—what
did you give up and what did you gain? It is likely that the major reason was positive, but the move meant leaving friends and neighbors,
perhaps your favorite shopping area or a club or place of worship in
which you were involved. Marriage, pursuing education and parent-
hood are other examples of life decisions that entail advantages and
sacrifices, requiring compromise. It takes a while to realize the full
benefits of a transition and gain perspective over the losses.

Although you may be considering this move for significant reasons, such as wanting more assistance with the upkeep of your
home or because you are planning for your future health needs,
there are many reasons that may cause you to hesitate. It is important for you to decide how the gains and losses measure up for you.
Do the gains outweigh the losses?

First think of the positive aspects. Moving offers many positive opportunities, such as a stimulating new environment and the potential for improvement in your quality of life. Many people who move appreciate the extra help and the provision of some services, such as not having to prepare meals. Women, in particular, may be tired of the day to day concern about what to cook for dinner. After moving, some express a feeling that they have finally retired since they don't have to worry about a household for the first time in their adult lives. The social atmosphere of a retirement community offers the chance to meet people with similar interests and to take part in leisure and recreational activities that are difficult to enjoy when you live in your own home.

When you become a resident of a retirement community you give up the freedom to make some decisions about daily life. Most community settings have some scheduled routines, for example, set meal times or housekeeping days. By the nature of communal living, retirement community settings offer less privacy. If you own your home outright, you may not be used to facing a monthly rental or fee. Remember that although you may not have paid rent, you did have taxes and insurance to pay on your home at set intervals.

Some people who move to retirement communities dislike the age homogeneity, and miss the stimulation of neighbors of varying ages. However, the opportunity to be around people of similar age is as an advantage, with the likelihood of common interests and the chance to grow old together. Finally, you may feel less energetic in approaching this move and may have more doubts and anxieties than in previous relocations. Focusing on the difficulties can be immobilizing and could delay your decision. As you evaluate your hesitations, think about whether you could overcome these concerns. Your analysis of the costs and benefits of moving will help you figure out whether you want to progress with further exploration of the moving decision.

In this chapter you carefully considered what you wanted and needed in a new home. The next section will help you prepare to make the move.

SECTION II

The Move

CHAPTER 5

Preparing for the Move

If you are like most people, you have relocated at least several times in your life. However, it may have been many years since your last move and the details have faded. Planning is essential whether you are moving a short or long distance. There is a lot to do, and you may not have as much time as you wish you had. Don't panic! You can accomplish it all if you take one step at a time. This chapter will help you with the details of preparing to move.

Pacing

It helps a great deal if you develop some type of timetable so that you don't become overwhelmed with details and discouraged before you even begin. We encourage you to get a notebook and write down all of the things you have to do. Time is a relative thing and you should not feel rushed into making decisions quicker than you feel comfortable. You should also not drag it out to the point that it consumes all of your time and thoughts.

The length of time taken to make the decision to move and the selection of a new home varies a great deal. Some people like the opportunity to plan several years ahead of the move and make an informed choice of residence. In some situations, after making the choice, the person is on a waiting list, delaying the opportunity to move until there is a vacancy in the community. For others, a downturn of health or an unexpected change of circumstances requires a quicker decision.

It is wise to think ahead and organize your plans when you have some idea of when you will be moving. We recommend that you consider the different tasks that you will need to complete before you make your move, and then think about a reasonable time table for your progress. These tasks include arranging for moving your belongings, sorting through your belongings, distributing possessions that you will not be taking with you, selling your home or giving notice on your lease, communicating your new address to your friends and business contacts, closing your old residence and making arrangements for your comfort and convenience in your new home.

There can be much work involved in leaving your current home and you may discover that there are hidden opportunities in this "work." If you can, take the time to savor the chance to get ready for your new home. Despite the time you have, it is essential that you pace activities and take care of yourself throughout the process. You need to plan for adequate rest, your usual exercise and a balanced diet with regular meals. Getting too tired is courting illness, and there cannot be a worse time to feel any other way than your best. A last minute rush creates a sense of panic and exhaustion. Fatigue is an enemy of sound decision making.

You might want to develop a written plan for each period before your move. Consider the event like an architect would in designing a building, with objectives for each phase known in advance. That way you know whether you are completing all the necessary tasks on schedule. If you are behind in your time table, you may want to reorganize so that you have the opportunity to catch up later. Be realistic and realize that you can't accomplish your move quickly if you do it correctly.

Planning to Move Your Belongings

When most people think of moving, they envision the task as simply the physical transfer of their belongings. While this is not all there is to a move, you will need to plan for this essential activity. If you are going to use a professional mover (and your life will be considerably less complicated if you choose to do so), contact several moving companies in your area early. Generally, most moving companies are busiest during the summer months and at the end of each month. Avoid those times if possible. Costs will vary depending on whether you will be moving to another state or close by. In-state moving charges are generally by the hour, whereas out-of-state movers charge by the weight and distance. We recommend that you obtain at least two cost estimates for the move. Make sure that you are asking the moving companies to bid on the same services. Specify what you want prices for, such as packing your belongings, transporting the belongings, storage during transit, etc.

The moving company will send a representative (sometimes called a relocation counselor) to meet with you in your home. All of the major companies will provide you with helpful information about how to prepare and what to expect from your move. Unless they own a suitable vehicle, family or friends helping you move will need to arrange to rent a truck or van.

Sorting Possessions

Sorting through possessions and deciding what to do with them is a major task. This part of the move is the most time consuming and physically and emotionally taxing. Some things will bring back cherished memories. You must sort through all of your belongings and decide whether to take them with you, give them to family or friends, or sell or donate them to charity. If you are like most people, and if you have been living in your home for some time, many items are stashed away in your attic, basement or closets. These objects have been out of sight and mind for years and will bring back both happy and painful memories. If you are physically able, it is best to do this yourself because only you know the meaning of your possessions.

You may view the sorting of your possessions as a daunting task at first. However, this is your chance to clear out those things you no longer need and rediscover the treasures that have gone unnoticed for years. Undoubtedly, you have accumulated a considerable houseful of belongings. You need to ask yourself two important questions:

1) How do I simplify?

2) How do I get rid of things I no longer want?

Your task will be to decide what to keep and what to do with those items you do not want to keep. Most people seek simplicity at this stage in their lives. Some ideas about priorities from experienced movers may help. Consider those items that you need for your comfort (a favorite chair or cozy quilt), those that have special meaning to you (family photos or gifts with sentimental value), and those that will help you recreate your home, (a coffee pot or favorite books). Also, decide which items you definitely don't need, either because of the available space or the future uselessness of the item. Regard the process of sorting as an opportunity to reflect on your life and the accomplishments of those dear to you, your interests over the years and the history of your family. Most people experience a tremendous sense of accomplishment and relief knowing that they have put their affairs in order and have accounted for their belongings.

In most situations you will be moving to smaller quarters with less storage capacity and have to consider what items you most want to keep. It is a good idea to construct a template drawn to scale of the new apartment. Most communities offer floor plans of the units drawn to scale; these are usually included in a brochure about the community. This will help you plan where you want to place large items of furniture. It will also help you figure out if your furniture can fit into your new home. You won't need some things, such as garden equipment or major cooking utensils, in the new setting; this will guide some sorting decisions. You will need certain possessions for your physical comfort or for sentimental reasons and these should be kept to create your new home. Think about what belongings are essential to make you feel at home.

The job of sorting is the least amenable to delegate to friends or family members who want to help you. You may want to decide what to keep and how to distribute those possessions that you don't retain. While it is important for you to make the decisions about your belongings, family and friends who want to be involved can help by toting boxes and other belongings for your review and by packing or distributing those items you want to pass on to others.

We encourage you to play a role in sorting your possessions. Our experience with people who were unable to participate in this process shows that they have more difficulty reconciling their losses. They are the most unhappy with their moves and continue to be plagued by questions about the whereabouts of certain treasured items, as described by this woman:

> They did rid me of a lot of things that I might have wanted to hold onto. During my illness I wasn't able to make some decisions that had to be made, so everything was

put into an estate sale. I would have liked to delay or had some input . . . there would've been four girls to whom I would love to have given something to. My wedding, my own wedding pictures, I don't know where they are along with so many other things.

Distributing Possessions

You may give special thought to the distribution of your possessions, particularly those that have family significance. It is quite satisfying to decide to whom you want to give a beloved piece that has value or special meaning. This is your chance to consider who in the next generation would most appreciate and cherish the item and its meaning to you and your family. As you sort through your possessions, you will get ideas about what to do with each. Parting with significant belongings will be a good experience if you can identify someone who will treasure it as much as you did. You may have a dear friend or family member interested in the history of a certain belonging who would be honored to be the new custodian for you. It often surprises people to find the response they get when they give a piece of particular value to them, to someone who is thrilled to be thought of as an exceptional friend. One woman, who gave her most treasured possessions to her grandnieces, reported:

> I'm glad the kids got what they wanted. Trish writes to me and says, "Aunt Dana, you just have to come and see what I've done with the goodies you gave me." It means a lot to them, they like it and ask questions about the old times. They're so interested in what went on when we

were small. I gave her my old dinner service and some beautiful pictures and she wanted to know all about them.

Distributing your possessions may include throwing items away, selling some or giving them to charity. You may want to have a garage or yard sale as an expedient way to get rid of many possessions. However, it takes considerable time and effort to have a garage sale and some people find it becomes a major chore. There are combined garage sales where several households sell their unwanted possessions together, and there are also books on planning and carrying out a garage sale. Some people make it their business to help with this task and may contract with you to take care of it totally in return for a commission on the sales.

If you have valuable pieces of furniture or art you may want to call an antique dealer and sell some pieces individually. If you don't want the trouble of selling items separately, many dealers will give you a set price for everything. This is what a woman had to say:

> When I think of the sale things, if I would have had time, if I would have been physically able, I could have gotten big prices for some of my things by having antique people come in. And I have to look back on the sales, I keep avoiding that, to see what those things brought. But if I would have had time and the health to do it, I could have benefited a lot more. But then, greed doesn't get you anything either. So somebody will enjoy it. I should have worked at that a long time before.

If you elect to give some of your things to charity, call several well in advance. Ask the staff about the following matters:

1) Do they pick items up from your home?

2) What items will they take?

3) How much notice do they need?

If you plan to take a charitable deduction for purposes of reporting your gift to the Internal Revenue Service, you should itemize all of your gifts carefully and place a monetary value on each. It is even advisable to take a picture of some pieces you give away in the event that a challenge is made about the value of your gifts. The decision of what the value should be is yours because charities generally avoid evaluating the monetary value of any item. They only issue a receipt that they have accepted the merchandise.

Some charities will decline certain items. For example, if they are unable to sterilize a king size mattress, they may not remove it from your home. Charities have become leery of being dumping grounds, and assess each item before accepting it. So it is wise to know in advance what their rules are for accepting merchandise to avoid disappointment with the resultant problem of having to dispose of a large item at the last moment.

Owning many books may present a particular challenge. After you cull out those books that you wish to keep, call your local library, high school, college or university. Many now have programs called "Friends of the Library" to enhance their collections. You can take a charitable contribution for your gift of books, and you will feel good knowing others are enjoying your personal library.

Continuity and Familiarity

The chance to move may stimulate a desire to wipe the slate clean and start over. For some people this impulse is overwhelming, and probably not the best idea. It is tempting to get rid of everything, but stop and consider if there is anything that would help you to maintain a sense of continuity and familiarity. Although a great deal of planning focuses on the tasks before the actual move, the greatest challenge is recreating a home. While the elements of home vary, most of us can identify features that will help this process.

Allow yourself sufficient time so that you will not give away things that you will later regret, but also put yourself into the frame of mind that you are moving to smaller quarters and will need considerably less. Small apartments appear crowded and cluttered with furniture designed for a house. Unless you are sentimentally attached to your couch and overstuffed chairs, now is the time to change them to simple furniture that will fit better in a smaller space. However, even if you decide to get all new furniture, keep some pieces that are special to you and will provide continuity, and the warmth of the familiar.

Sometimes a married couple will differ in their views about what they should take with them and what they should give away.

A man told this story:

> My wife and I would never agree on what furniture we
> should take with us. She wanted to take some large pieces
> that just wouldn't fit and would look terrible in the small-
> er rooms we were moving to. So, finally, after many argu-
> ments I persuaded her to let a neutral person help us. I
> hired an interior decorator who helped enormously. My
> wife now agrees that our huge sofa would have been
> totally out of place.

Some items in your home may belong to your children who now
have homes of their own but have managed to leave behind their
school yearbooks, memorabilia and college notes. If your adult children live nearby, invite them over to sort through their things. If they
live a distance from you, get a supply of boxes or an inexpensive
trunk, and ship their things to them.

This is what one woman said:

> After I made the decision to move from where I was mar-
> ried and lived for over 40 years, and raised my daughters,
> I went out and bought four inexpensive foot lockers. I put
> in all of the stuff that belonged to each of my four kids
> and shipped off all the term papers, school books, pressed
> flowers from proms and other things they refused to take
> to their own homes after they started their own families.
> You have no idea how good it felt to be rid of all of their
> stuff.

You will experience a sense of relief and freedom when you have cleared away your possessions. It distills your possessions to fewer select items. The opportunity to distribute heirlooms and enjoy the responses of the recipients while you are still alive is a satisfying thing to do. Interestingly, most people do not have feelings of sadness, but have a sense of accomplishment and relief for doing a difficult job. A woman expressed her feelings:

> I burned all my bridges behind me. All my treasures that I've had for years. A gorgeous solid oak dining set, that was 60 years old, that my granddaughter has. I wanted her to have it. She'll treasure it. So that's all taken care of.

The task of sorting is not easy, and this is what another woman had to say:

> I finally arrived at the point not to look too long at anything, to just let it go. I had our wedding gift dishes in the basement, never been opened since we had lived in that house. Beautiful stuff that I don't suppose I used more than a dozen times. And I had saved all my grocery sacks and papers before the recycling deal. And of course all the jars, I used to can my own food, I had so many things in boxes. Things from years ago.

Tying Up Loose Ends

Preparing to move to a retirement community can be an opportunity to tie up the loose ends of the past and discard unnecessary trappings. Dealing with this preparation before failing health or physical ability precludes your involvement allows you to execute some control over this process.

Another benefit of moving is the chance to reorganize by clearing out one household and establishing another. When faced with the legal transactions associated with the sale of a home, many people take the opportunity to get other affairs in order. These include such legal matters as making certain that your durable powers of attorney (for finances and health care) are up to date and reflect your current wishes. Going through your records may stimulate you to rewrite your will or consolidate your investments. While the tasks of moving may seem unending, you can take advantage of this state of limbo to get your affairs in order.

Consider having copies made of family pictures so that you can distribute them to all of your children and other relatives. This way, you can share these priceless possessions with your family. As you go through your things, it will remind you of what you want to do. As your memories occur, take the time to write thoughts down in your notebook. When you get settled again, a wonderful gift you can give your children, grandchildren, nieces and nephews is the stories of their family. You will find it fun to do, and if writing is difficult for you, ask for a tape recorder as a gift and chronicle your life verbally.

Selling Your Home

Part of the moving process may involve selling your home. The length of time to sell your home will depend on the current market in your area, and will involve preparing your home for sale. Finding a good real estate agent early in the process is most beneficial, as she or he can advise you about all aspects of the sale and can help you with your preparations. Some people attempt to sell their homes themselves. This can work if you are in a market in which there are fewer homes than people wanting to buy them. However, keep in mind that it is difficult to be objective about a home you love, and you may overlook its faults in much the same way as you do with your old friends and family members. Also remember that it will take considerable time and effort to show your home to strangers, and their remarks about your house may insult you or hurt your feelings. A professional middle person provides the buffer between buyer and seller. Buyers usually do not feel comfortable making comments or expressing their feelings in front of a seller unless they feel the price is a bargain or so low that they are willing to overlook its defects. Also, many states have disclosure laws about the condition of the house and neighborhood and an agent can help you with these requirements.

Because you will want maximum exposure to buyers, it would be wise to list with a broker who subscribes to a multiple listing service (MLS) in your community. The MLS is a database that describes all of the houses for sale. It is available to most agents and is usually controlled by the local affiliate of the National Association of Realtors. The MLS listing includes a description of the house, and other information, such as when the house is available, the existing financing, whether the seller will take the down payment in installments and other requirements made by the seller.

As home computers continue to gain in popularity, they are changing the way real estate is marketed. A real estate office with the capability of offering electronic information can tap future buyers with a home computer and give them detailed descriptions with pictures of the home and its neighborhood. You may want to seek these services to reach a larger group of prospective buyers.

Seek a competent agent who knows your area and the value of houses in your neighborhood. Your home probably represents your largest single asset, and a good sale will provide the nest egg that you will need for the next phase of your life. So proceed with caution and choose a sensitive and caring agent who understands your situation and whom you trust to help you with this important task.

How do you go about finding a competent agent? If possible, take the time to go to open houses of other properties in your area. Talk with the listing agent and observe how she or he talks to prospective clients. Is the agent knowledgeable and enthusiastic about the property? Ask friends, neighbors or relatives who recently sold a house for a recommendation. Interview more than one possible agent.

You should consider asking the following questions when you meet with a prospective agent:

1) How many homes have you sold during the past year? Where are they? Did they sell for close to the asking price?

2) Are you willing to give me the names of three of your former clients?

3) Are you willing to cooperate with another agent if a future buyer has an agent?

4) What is the minimum length of a listing you will accept?

5) What commission do you expect, and is it negotiable?

Before signing your home listing with an agent, be sure to telephone the two or three most recent home sellers of each agent to ask if they were in any way unhappy and if they would list with that agent again. The time you spend before listing your house will save you possible aggravation and disappointment later.

When you have selected the agent, make certain there is a written agreement that details everything she or he has promised to do. Most realty firms have printed forms, but remember that you do not have to accept all that is written on them, nor do you have to limit your agreement to their standard form. Take care before you sign. You may want to work with a real estate attorney who will represent your interests in negotiations with the realtor and throughout the sale transaction.

Be fair to the agent if you expect diligent work from him or her. For example, there is a cost to preparing the listing and for that reason most agents will not accept a listing for under three months. The more knowledgeable you are the better value you will receive from your agent. It may help to read some books on real estate sales from the public library to understand the terminology and know what to expect.

Another service that a good real estate agent will provide for you is advice on what you need to do to get your home ready for a sale. Generally, houses sell quicker and for a better price if they are in good condition. A coat of paint and new carpets will transform a shabby house. If you don't want to spruce up your home, then it usually will be listed as a "fixer upper" for a reduced sales price. Only you can decide if it is worth the investment of making reasonable changes as you prepare to sell your home.

Although newspaper advertising appeals to sellers, realtors point out that it is the MLS that brings buyers. Some agents will insist on hosting an open house so that people can stop in. It does bring forth sightseers and neighbors, but it is the best way for the community to know of the availability of your home. You will want to keep all of your valuables under lock and key because there is no way that even the most conscientious realtor can provide security.

Being Careful

Each year thousands of seniors are victims of swindles that rob them of their savings. It will be a matter of public record that you have sold your home, including the price. You can expect to receive calls with advice on how to invest your money from representatives of various financial companies trying to sell you everything from stocks and bonds to other real estate. You must be certain that the investment advice you receive is sound, and protects your interests.

You need to have a trusted financial advisor and we suggest that you obtain the services of one before the decision to sell your home. Do not give out information over the telephone to someone you do not know. Remember the old adage: If something sounds too good to be true, it is!

Many older adults have been financially victimized by people who won their trust and then claimed to be financial advisors. Educate yourself so that you are less likely to be victimized. Never invest in something that you don't understand. If anyone tells you there is absolutely no risk, be suspicious. Get additional opinions. Always demand a prospectus and review it carefully. If the person tells you that he or she is a broker, call your state securities regulator to find out if there has ever been disciplinary action against this broker. Con artists thrive on their good manners and looks so don't get yourself caught in one of their schemes.

Last Minute Details

Finally, you need to arrange to stop your utilities, your newspaper (or have it transferred to your new residence) and other services that you have engaged for your home. The utility companies will want a reading of the meters, so see that it is done. The telephone company will either transfer your service or disconnect it depending on how far away you are moving. The post office will give a free packet of helpful information, including a card to fill out with your forwarding address, which will remain in effect for one year from the date you ask to have your mail sent to the new address. You can renew this request if needed. You should also notify all of your friends, the subscription department for the magazines and periodicals you take, and any other business offices, including the

Department of Motor Vehicles (if you have a driver's license), the Social Security and Medicare offices. You should list all these details in your notebook so you can complete these small tasks.

In the next chapter we will discuss the day of the move itself. The more you have prepared, the easier the move will be.

CHAPTER 6

The Actual Move

In the last chapter we emphasized the importance of planning carefully for your move. If you have planned well, you will accomplish the actual move without a great deal of strain. Although as you read this it may sound unduly optimistic, our studies conclude that of all the phases of moving, the physical move itself is the easiest because you can accomplish it quickly with the help of family, friends and/or professional movers.

Moving day, with its flurry of activity and the seemingly endless tasks, is the day that most people think about when they contemplate moving. In reality, this is only one in a series of days that is part of the moving process. There are many things that you can do to make your moving day go smoothly, such as hiring qualified helpers, planning the steps necessary to close one home and open another, ensuring that your essentials (personal items, comfortable clothing, medications, favorite foods) are handy, and having an idea of where you want the different items delivered.

Taking Care of Yourself

Don't forget to take care of your own needs for rest, food, refreshment and relaxation in the midst of all the excitement of moving. Try to maintain as many of your usual routines as possible, such as the time you usually go to bed, eat your meals and other essential activities. Pace yourself. If you let the sense of urgency force you to abandon your carefully laid out time frame, you may find yourself suffering from fatigue or from health problems just when you need your strength most.

Moving Your Possessions

Now that you have made the decision of what you will keep and move, you will need either to pack your belongings or supervise the packing done by others. There are some tips that professional movers offer. First, be certain that you pack your medications and toiletry items carefully and securely. Also make certain that medications you take daily remain with you so you won't have to unpack them immediately when you arrive at your destination.

If you are planning to do some packing yourself, start packing a few boxes each day. You will need to either purchase boxes from the moving company, which can be expensive, or collect boxes from your grocery store. If you do that, be certain that the boxes are clean and sturdy. The manager will usually be happy to help you and tell you when the largest supply is available. Some moving companies will not insure boxes that their professionals have not packed. Ask about that in advance. It may be advisable to have a professional pack your most precious breakable items, while you or your helpers could handle books and other easy to pack items. If you do pack china or record albums, remember that professional movers always place these items on end vertically instead of stacking them flat.

Pack your possessions on a room by room basis. It is usually best not to mix items from different rooms in one box. Wrap small items carefully so they don't get lost. Some movers recommend brightly colored tissue paper for wrapping small items so you don't throw them out inadvertently with the packing paper. As you complete each box, either label it with the name of the room in which it will be going, or color code to match each room and box. It is helpful to label each box with a summary of the contents.

You should not allow anyone other than someone you trust to handle irreplaceable papers, fine jewelry or collections that you treasure or that have high monetary value. Although seldom, accidents and fires have happened in moving vans. You should not take the risk of losing something that is truly irreplaceable if you or a trusted friend or family member can transport it. You cannot ship hazardous materials, including nail polish and remover, aerosol cans, cleaning fluids or matches, because of the danger of fire. These items have no place in a moving van.

Some professional movers will take your plants, but most will not accept liability for their well-being. Plants mean different things to people, so if you have a plant or two that have been part of your family for a long while and you want to take them with you, prepare the plants for the move too. It is wise to prune before the move so recovery will have taken place before the shock of adjusting to a new environment. Place the plant in a sturdy carton and water it well allowing excess water to drain. Then put a large plastic bag over it with some air holes to keep it moist and warm during its move. Sometimes it's easier to take and transport cuttings from plants instead of a heavy potted plant.

Don't overlook one important detail. Most movers will not unload your shipment at the destination until you either pay or arrange to meet their charges. Before the move, make certain that you understand what you will owe the movers and how you can pay them.

Asking for Help

You can delegate the tasks of moving day, unlike many early tasks in the moving process, to willing helpers. This is a good time to take friends and family up on their offers of assistance. Because you can't be in two places simultaneously, list what your friends and family can do for you and help them assist you by being specific about your wishes.

Saying Goodbye

It is surprising how many people say that when it comes to the time to bid farewell to their home, they find that it is not as difficult as they had anticipated. However, others feel great sadness when leaving their home and neighborhood. Each person says goodbye in a different way. Consider how you would prefer to leave your home. Some people visit neighbors, wishing them well, giving them their new addresses and phone numbers, and inviting them to visit when they are settled in. Others prefer to leave unobtrusively and bid private farewells to a few select friends.

A wide range of memories fills most homes—the joys and challenges of the family and the experiences of many years. You may want to take a moment in each room and in the garden to reflect on your memories and say goodbye. Some people enjoy having pictures of the various rooms and areas of their home as a way of treasuring the memories contained therein. This is a time of ending and you may want to note its passing.

Unpacking in Your New Home

Whether you rely on friends and family to transfer your possessions or you hire a professional mover, you have to decide what will go where in advance. If you have made a template of the new rooms, you will know in advance where the heavy furniture will go. Discuss your plan with the movers so that they may place the heavy items upon delivery.

Just as you had a plan for your packing, have a timetable and plan for your unpacking. As you have labeled each box, you know what is in it and can decide what you need first. At this phase in the moving process it is important to remember that it will take time to accomplish your goals. It is overwhelming to look around a room and see many boxes you have to unpack. Set reasonable goals for yourself and allow the time necessary to get settled into your new home. There are additional matters to attend to, such as getting to know the routines and how to get your meals and other necessities. Intersperse your unpacking with your beginning involvement in the community.

Now that you have arrived in the new home you chose, the next few chapters will help you settle in to your new life and become an active member of your new community.

SECTION III

Settling In

CHAPTER 7

Nesting

Now is your chance to claim your new home as your own. How do you know when the place you live is your home? Is it when your special things are all displayed again? Or when you're curled up with a good book in your favorite chair and hear music filtering through the rooms of your home? Everyone has a different idea about what it means to be "home," but many agree that there are four basic ingredients to feeling at home. First, there is a sense of interpersonal warmth and connection with others, whether they are neighbors, guests, family or friends. In other words, others are welcome to share your place. Second, there is a sense of physical comfort and relaxation. Third, you are willing to invest energy and effort in the physical environment, such as cleaning, arranging things and decorating it. Finally, you feel the freedom to be yourself with the special combination of license and privacy. You can express your true self and feel secure that you are not on public view. As you create your new home, consider how you can set the stage for feeling settled.

Creating a Sense of Home

A sense of warmth can help an apartment feel more like a home. For many, this means sharing the space with friends or family. This is particularly true for people who have always opened their homes and hosted others. The sound of the voices of those to whom we are close makes a lonely space warm up quickly. This is how one woman defined home:

> I think it's a home when people feel very welcome. You know, they know they can go in the bathroom and if they want to use powder or an aspirin, take a tissue or anything else they just feel comfortable doing it. Because you have opened up your home to them and they know it. This is home for me and my friends know it. It's the place where I'm surrounded by love.

When you first move in, the chaos of the unpacking process may preclude your having visitors. It is helpful to create spaces to live in as quickly as possible, such as your sleeping area, dining area and relaxing area. If your chairs are set up in the living room and your kettle is unpacked, it is much easier to stop and have a cup of tea or coffee with a friend who drops by to see you. Once you feel a little settled, invite someone special over for a short visit—choose someone who doesn't mind your unfinished work and will lift your spirits and energize you. The admiration and encouragement of a friend or family member may be just the thing to keep you going and make you feel at home.

Making Yourself Comfortable

Creating physical comfort means personalizing your environment with cozy furniture, music and possessions that convey a sense of belonging, such as pictures on the wall and important souvenirs. A man gave his prescription for physical comfort:

> Of course, enough furniture to be comfortable. Fully carpeted so you can run around barefoot. I think a home fits you, it should have enough beds, bedrooms and bathrooms to suit your family. We've always been pretty lucky in that respect.

Many of your early efforts will focus on setting up your apartment for your personal convenience and as a reflection of your unique tastes. Important decisions at this time include how you want to use the space and arrange your belongings and how you would like to decorate and personalize your new home. In the first few weeks, you will get a sense of the patterns of light and traffic in the new space and ideas will come to you about the optimal arrangement of furnishings. Again, planning is important, as illustrated by this woman:

It doesn't look like home yet, it doesn't look like I want it to yet. I'm just kind of playing with something, maybe I'd kind of like a red geranium over there. And I have ordered some green drapes, a cactus green, which will be kind of a soft green. It's so light in the morning, that I just wake up at the light. So I thought I'd get something a little darker, and I would love to find a bookcase to put in here somewhere. And maybe a new desk there, get one that has drawers, then I could put my own personal papers down there. You know so many times you get a lot of cards. And then when you want to find people you can't find them. So I put my little board up there. And I put my clothes in here so I can air them out a bit. The thing is, you have to have a place for everything.

This woman has illustrated an important point. As you have probably moved to less space than you previously had, it is essential that you organize it to meet your needs. You are not alone in wanting a place for everything. There are businesses that design furniture to meet the storage needs of the apartment dweller. There are small decorative trunks and suitcases that make attractive storage. A wicker picnic basket, for example, is an inexpensive way to keep sewing materials. An armoire can store your television or music system unobtrusively. Keep storage in mind as you look at what you brought with you and use some of your furniture imaginatively for purposes other than before.

You may find that you gave away some items that you had not anticipated needing, such as occasional tables, an iron, ironing board or a mirror. You may find that you want some new items to help make your apartment your home. These may include furniture, as illustrated in the following quotation by this woman:

> You would think that I don't like them, but I haven't put up pictures because I didn't get exactly the right furniture. This table needs to go and I need two end tables which will mean recentering that wall. And this isn't right either, I'm just dragging my heels trying to find the end tables I want and the pictures just stand in the corner. When they are up it will be more of a home to me.

A few safety and decorating tips may help you. First, safety should be your prime concern. Therefore, be careful that you anchor all scatter rugs to the floor. Remember that the rubber backing from bathroom rugs wears out with washing and drying in a heated automatic dryer. Glass-top coffee tables can pose a danger should someone fall nearby. You and others could trip over electrical cords, so consider placing lamps and appliances near electrical outlets. Chairs with arms help people raise and lower themselves. Furniture seats should be at least 19 inches from the floor for the same reason. Get dining room chairs that are light enough to be easy to move. And remember to place your furniture a few inches away from baseboard heaters.

Comfortable furnishings, pleasant decorations, plants and flowers characterize a living environment. You create a warm and inviting apartment by displaying prized possessions and by surrounding yourself with familiar and special objects. To avoid a cluttered appearance, professional interior decorators usually group small objects instead of scattering them throughout the room. You can create a cozy appearance with two chairs and a small nearby table on which to place a book, a drink or some decorative objects. Well-worn and loved heirlooms such as furniture, quilts, samplers and pictures convey a sense of comfort and home. Possessions with a significant history reflect personal identity. A woman expresses herself:

> I took the furniture that I thought I needed here, maybe I didn't make very good choices, but anyway, I feel at home with it. It's junky, but I feel at home with it. That table, I was raised on. We kids all sat around that in 1900 to study, you know. And the bedroom set, everybody said, "Oh get a new set." Well I didn't, I brought that. And I took a quilt that my mother made for me, it's one of these patchwork deals. I think it's very pretty, I love it.

Possessions offer an opportunity to express yourself and let others know who you are. Another woman describes it like this:

> Being a teacher I've always had so many books in my life. To me it's nice, they make me feel good. I've lived with them for so long, an accumulation starting back when I was in high school, many of them are out of print. Then I have a lot of records too. My sister-in-law says, "Oh, why do you take your stereo along?" Well, you know, it has a lot of records that I've had a lot of fun getting and sometimes you can put a whole bunch on and when it's lonely it's kind of nice to have those things.

Investing Energy

When you invest the energy and thought into arranging and modifying your apartment, you are asserting your own personality and taste. Investment of time and energy in the environment is a third critical element of home. Home is what you make it. The creation of a home is an active endeavor. A woman conveyed her enthusiasm for homemaking:

> I think a family taking interest in the home is the one thing. Now, I have always kept the house up, and I've always done my own work. I've always wall papered my own houses, I've always painted anything that had to be done. You've just got to keep at it all the time. I just like to do those things. There's nothing about a house that I don't like to do.

There are unlimited opportunities to invest energy in your new home; you probably wish that there would be less to do! Though rental apartments have been cleaned before occupancy, many people feel more at home after they have cleaned and put new paper on the shelves. Depending on the policies of the community, you may be able to paint or carpet your new home. For many, the effort of setting up the home is sufficient to feel that one has invested energy in the new environment.

You will find that unpacking and arranging possessions are activities that will occupy you for months after the move. Particularly if you did an incomplete job of sorting your possessions before moving, you will need to continue with this endeavor.

Appreciating Your Freedom

Finally, having the freedom to be yourself is an essential element in the definition of home. This means an expectation of both privacy and license and a recognition of a boundary between home and the outside world.

As you become familiar with the norms of your new community, you will know how sociable your neighbors are. If your privacy is important to you, find ways to express your preferences early. For example, if neighbors drop by at an inconvenient time, you may thank them for their visit, say that you are busy at this time, but ask whether you could join them for the next meal. There are many opportunities to socialize, and it is important for you to ensure that you have the privacy you desire.

Minimizing Negative Features

Even if you had the opportunity to design your own home, you would discover flaws that must be corrected. This may be even more of an issue when you did not have the opportunity to design your own apartment. As you consider your new home, are there any features that are problematic for you, such as a bathtub that is too difficult to get into, or a lack of privacy from a particular window? These are readily and easily corrected with a secure grab bar and clever window dressing. It may help you to settle in if you can identify any small modifications you can make to enhance your comfort and minimize negative features. Report any difficulties with your apartment you identify to the administration. We will be discussing in later chapters how to let others know about your needs.

We have covered some important points in helping you to begin to settle into your new environment, beginning with your efforts to make the most of your physical comfort, to recreate important elements of your home and to personalize your environment. By investing energy, thought and time in arranging and personalizing your apartment, you will improve your physical comfort and express your personality. You will find the freedom to be yourself in the ways you decorate your home for both comfort and privacy.

Your next task is how you work out the logistics and take advantage of the programs in your new community. We will give you some ideas and advice in Chapter 8.

Working Out Logistics

In the last chapter we discussed how to claim your new home as your own. Your physical comfort extends beyond the walls of your private apartment to the surrounding retirement community and its neighborhood and includes the ability to meet your daily needs. A significant component of settling in is working out the logistics of life, such as where and how to shop, how to send and receive mail, how to do laundry, how to get around in the neighborhood and what to do in case of an emergency.

Making the Most of Your New Home

Settling in also means figuring out how to make the most of your new home. Before you moved you probably received some information about the routines, services and programs of the retirement community. If you have not already received orientation materials, ask a staff member to provide you with pertinent information and a tour of the entire facility. Write down any questions you might have so that you can ask staff or neighbors.

Moving disrupts many familiar networks and if you moved from a distant neighborhood, the task of settling in will include learning the resources and peculiarities of the local community. If you are new to the area, you can get general information from the Chamber of Commerce. Senior Information and Assistance Hotlines are excellent resources regarding services and programs in the area and can be found in the State Government section of the phone book. Subscribe to a local newspaper and visit the library for more information about your new setting.

Getting Needed Information

There are other important things to learn about your new home. These include information about meals and housekeeping. You also need to learn how to get involved in the recreational activities, where to shop or bank and where to do your personal laundry. You will want to learn about the transportation system—both public and the services provided by the facility. Depending on what is available, you may find that you will need to adjust your routines.

There are many different sources of information to help you adjust. Most communities have a Resident Handbook, or another form of printed material about their services. Request copies of the Resident Handbook, activity calendars, menus and recent newsletters so that you can get an idea of what is going on in the community. Meal and housekeeping services are a part of the daily life of the community, and information about these important services is easy to find.

In general, the more your needs are held in common with others, the easier it will be to find and get what you want. For example, if group transportation is available, the facility will tell you about van trips to shopping areas and group activities. For individual activities, such as attending a civic club meeting or going out to a restaurant, you may find another person with a similar interest to share the taxi. The greatest challenge is meeting requirements that are unique to you and unknown by other residents, such as trying to figure out which bus to take to a specific location. You may have to consult an outside agency for advice in these situations.

Many retirement communities offer a variety of formal activities both within the community and as organized excursions. There is usually an activity calendar published monthly. Musical and theatrical performances and trips to places of interest can be sources of considerable enjoyment. Games, such as bingo and bridge, are popular. Other group endeavors, such as educational or religious classes, provide forums for group discussion on topics of interest. There may be formal projects or programs organized by the recreational staff, or they may happen spontaneously in small groups through the efforts of your neighbors.

You may not want regular involvement in the activities of the community, continuing your involvement in previous activities and interests. Or you may prefer to limit your social involvement only to meal times. The choice is yours.

Meeting Daily Living Needs

In a retirement community, one of the first things you need to learn about is how to meet daily living needs. When and where to go for your meals is essential knowledge. In most retirement communities the dining hours are set at regular times and the menu may be posted in advance, commonly in the dining room area. Meal provision is a reason that many move, as described by this woman, who appreciated the convenience:

> Just like the lady said how glad she was when she came in from a busy day and she didn't have to get dinner. I'll never forget that, because I know just how she felt. It makes a lot of sense.

While the ready availability of meals is an advantage to many, some people find it difficult to adjust to the schedule of meal times and limited choices. The same woman quoted above discusses the disadvantages of communal meals:

The regimen was hard because you live so many years by doing things whenever you want to do things; that seems to me to be the worst thing. I have to get out of bed earlier to be ready for breakfast. You have to be at a certain place at a certain time. And I think that they should have a substitute when you can't eat what is on the menu.

You may prefer preparing your own breakfast rather than getting up early to dress and be ready for the communal meal. You may want to stock favorite fruits, cookies or beverages in your own kitchen. Eating in one place all the time can get monotonous.

Part of your orientation to meal times should also include whether the community has open or assigned seating for all meals, or some meals. It can be embarrassing to sit at someone else's table and not know that you have displaced a person whose routine includes sitting at a particular place. Some communities make it a point to encourage open seating to avoid ownership of a place; others encourage dining with the same table companions. Either way, it is important that you know what the customs are.

Many communities provide housekeeping services weekly, including changing bed linens and towels. This means that all you have to do is tidy up your apartment and not worry about the heavier tasks such as vacuuming or cleaning the bathroom. One woman put it this way:

I have all the room I need and I don't have to take care of it, because the dear housekeeper comes in. For the first time in 81 years, I'm a lady.

Doing the laundry is another routine you will need to learn about. Some retirement communities have individual laundry facilities in each apartment; others have laundry rooms available at no charge or with machines operated by coins. You may find that managing your own light washables in your apartment is easiest for you, and that by enlisting the help of family or friends for laundering heavier garments you will get along nicely.

Getting Help from Others

Moving into a community of others can be intimidating. You will feel like a newcomer, and assume that everyone else knows each other and is focusing on you. Chances are that there are others who feel the same way you do, perhaps some who have also moved recently, and remember the feelings of those first few days. You may be surprised by how willing others are to help. Many people take pride in their communities and are eager to let you in on the routines and services of your new home. Some communities have a welcoming committee to help you feel at ease and answer your questions. Take advantage of the goodwill of new neighbors if they offer to help. You will have a chance to return the favor to a newcomer in the future. Don't be afraid to approach staff if you are uncertain about how to obtain assistance. They are there to help you, and others before you have probably also wanted to know the answers to your questions. Most of the people we interviewed worked out their logistics with some advice from others in the community and with minimal assistance from their families. For example, a man who felt rejected when he sat at a place customarily occupied by someone else at breakfast learned to ask before he joined the group.

Sharing tasks, such as shopping, is another way that many people living in retirement communities help each other. Cooperative arrangements can be rewarding and easier on both you and a neighbor. You may not want to aid others, but you may also enjoy the opportunity to help others, as expressed by this woman:

> You do it automatically. You don't really realize what you are doing, but you get joy from helping somebody. I don't know, it's just being close to another human heart. There was a little woman who came from New Jersey, came out here, way out here, and I was sitting with her the other day, and she didn't know about the tickets on the bus. Little things like that, are things that you can fill someone in on. Things that they can get, and will help them, it's kind of nice.

Some people, such as this woman who wanted to help others, recognized her own limitations:

> Some of them are not well. And you try to help them. But what do you do, you don't know how to help them. Some of them keep calling all the time because they're so depressed and lonesome. You can get really involved if you're not careful. Not that you don't want to help them, but it isn't a responsibility that you know how to handle. And you shouldn't assume it anyway. You have to know your limitations.

It is important to point out that not everyone wants to help neighbors and you may question the appropriateness of doing so. One woman observed:

> The woman that lives across the hall, she's not old and decrepit, but she's a little woman, and her health is not good. And the woman she helps is a great big tall slender woman. And she gets her down on her chair, gets her down to the dining room at night and gets her up off the chair and gets her home at night. Now I'm sure she didn't move in here to be a nurse. I'm not going to be anybody's nurse. I'm sympathetic with them, yes, but I did not move here to be a nurse. I came in here to kind of be looked after myself.

One large challenge of living in a retirement community is learning to get along with many other people, particularly those who are aging and experiencing health changes. As a member of the community, you face the issue of give and take among your peers. For some, frequent exchanges and mutual assistance are desirable; others prefer to live more privately. It is important for you to achieve your own level of comfort with the demands of community life and figure out how you can contribute to the life of the community.

Arranging Transportation

Working out logistics extends beyond the walls of the retirement community to the surrounding vicinity. Transportation may be a significant barrier in accomplishing your regular chores and routines acceptably and efficiently. You may no longer drive or you may limit your driving to daylight hours. Lack of personal transportation may impose a restriction on your individual choice and your ability to explore and solve the problems of daily life independently. A man describes his difficulties with transportation:

> I don't feel as if I should be driving. I don't know, maybe I could, but I haven't since my surgery. If something happens, then the first thing they would say would be, "What on earth was he doing driving?"I haven't tried the bus because I have seen too many people get on the bus and inconvenience all the rest of the passengers and I don't want to do that. Another reason I haven't tried the bus is that it is too much of a job for me to walk any distance at all. I don't know the bus system well enough to know whether I could get within, well, the closest I know you can get to from here would be almost six or seven blocks and that's just too far for me.

Getting transportation independently may be a challenge for you. Taxi service may be expensive but necessary on occasion. When your family asks what you might like for your birthday or holidays, you could suggest taxi coupons for transportation. Depending on where your home is, public transportation may be readily accessible or it could be a problem for you particularly if you have impaired mobility or vision. It is sometimes difficult to figure out the routes and schedules. A call to your local bus service will give you the information that you need. You may find that your local public transportation has a service where all you have to do is tell them where you are and where you want to go. Even if you have difficulty in boarding and leaving, you should not feel awkward using public transportation. Bus drivers are able and willing to help those who need their assistance.

You may feel safer getting rides with others. Accept the offer for a ride, particularly when you know that the driver had planned to go to the same destination and you are going to share the event together, such as going to your place of worship or a club meeting. When you purchase some needed gasoline, you will be helping the driver simultaneously as she or he is accommodating you.

Most retirement communities own a van to help tenants accomplish their weekly shopping, banking and occasional health care visits. You can shop for groceries and household supplies during the excursions to malls. You may enjoy going to social events in the van, usually for an added fee. These excursions are a safe, well-planned service that can be a great help.

What to do in an Emergency

Your final logistical challenge is developing a plan for emergencies. Knowing how to get help and what to expect from staff is an important task as you settle into your new environment. Commonly, you will find emergency call switches in your bedroom and bathroom. In addition, there may be other safety measures. As an example, some communities ask residents to check in on a daily basis, or staff will call or visit to make sure they are all right. You may want to memorize and rehearse how to get help if you have a personal emergency.

It is important to know what you must do in a building emergency. Find out about the procedures to follow in case of fire or disaster by asking the staff. The construction of many newer buildings limits the spread of fire; therefore residents should remain in their rooms with the doors shut unless instructed to evacuate. Other communities require residents to evacuate in case of an emergency. It is essential that you become familiar with your primary and secondary evacuation routes, should you need to exit the building in the dark.

Working out the logistics of daily life is part of the settling in phase of moving. The primary outcome of this process will be a sense of personal comfort and assurance that you know how to get what you need without inconvenience to you or others. You will find that you can meet many of your needs within the retirement community, particularly if you choose the community carefully with your future needs in mind.

In the next chapter we will discuss other aspects of communal living, such as fitting in and making new friends.

Successful Adjustment

CHAPTER 9

Fitting In

We have discussed learning about your new environment, stressing the importance of finding information and seeking the help of others. Communal living communities have certain unique characteristics, particularly when compared to living in a single family home. They tend to have a shared identity, with expected ways of behaving. In this chapter we will help you gain some skills you may need to fit in with others.

Understanding the Environment

You will soon begin to form impressions of the community as a whole and of your fellow residents as individuals. Even before moving into the community, you may have begun to develop an understanding of the social and cultural environment. You may have known or had friends in the community before moving. You may also be familiar with the history and presence of the facility in the broader community.

Unlike single family homes or apartments, in communal living you will be part of a group where you will meet many of the same people and share routines day after day. Through learning what others expect from you, and how to behave, you will have a framework for getting along with others. You will get some of these norms of behavior through written policies or general announcements. For example, the administration will tell you what to do during a fire drill. Group pressure also plays a part in letting you know how to act, such as the dining room dress code or seating arrangements. Most behavioral norms include the generally recognized codes of etiquette of treating others with courtesy. You will find that it is not difficult to fit into the group's expectations and accept them.

Aging and Disability

After joining the community, it may strike you that the occupants share a similar age. This is most noticeable if you are used to a neighborhood with a wide range of ages. You will have to adjust to the density and intensity of the social environment. It may be the first time since school days that you find yourself eating every meal with so many other people. Because of the high volume of contact with others around meal times and other activities, it is important that you find ways to be alone when you want to be. You will find that most residents respect the privacy of others, so when you retreat to your apartment it is a sign that you feel like being by yourself. You will also find that most of your interactions with others take place in the public spaces or with a specific invitation to your private quarters.

A striking and sometimes distressing, feature of living with many older adults is having to face the disabilities and infirmities of others. People vary in their acceptance and tolerance of such changes. Your settling in and adjustment will depend on your ability to find the positive features of a group living environment and minimize those aspects that you may find less desirable.

Part of developing an understanding of the social environment is forming impressions of your fellow residents. You may even feel that some residents do not belong in a retirement community but in a nursing home. The following quotation illustrates the annoyance of one woman.

> I didn't move into a nursing home, but that's what I'm in. I was stupefied when I realized that there were people here that didn't have all their marbles.

Another woman elaborated further:

> I did not expect to see these walkers, maybe a cane or two but not to the extent that we have canes here. I didn't dream it would be like that. I figured that everybody was capable of getting around and fending for themselves, but that's not so. So in the beginning that was a little bit hard to take, and we're not the only ones. I've heard other people mention it. I may be that way tomorrow too, see. But I hope they'll do something with me so I won't bother anybody else.

Most communities screen applicants for eligibility to live independently. The criteria include functional ability, or the ability to manage activities of daily living, such as bathing, dressing and getting around. Many people harbor prejudices about those who use walkers, canes or wheelchairs. It is not uncommon for residents of a community to object to others who use such assistive devices. This is based on a misconception about the ability of that person. Walkers, wheelchairs and canes enable many people to be independent in their mobility and daily functioning. The Americans with Disabilities Act became law in 1991, and discriminating against people with disabilities is illegal. If you have concerns about the eligibility of members in your community, talk it over with the administration.

A Word for Single Men

A word here is in order if you are a single man. You may have more difficulty in discovering commonalities with the general resident population, most of whom are often women. This is what one man had to say:

> I just don't really have much in common with most of the people here. Course, like I say, they're all very friendly, I enjoy talking to them. But, well, what is there to talk about really, you know? Their symptoms and mine. Talk about the weather and world conditions.

There is no question that in many retirement communities the group activities tend to be of greatest interest to women residents. One male participant suggested a billiard table as a way of getting the men together in an activity. If being with so many women at once bothers you, choose to sit with other single men in the dining room and see if you can initiate conversations and activities that interest your peers. Another issue that many single men face is the potentially overwhelming romantic interest of women in their community. Because gender ratios tend to favor men, with many more women in proportion to men, some find that they have to deal with the complexity of managing the competition.

Getting Acquainted

Living in a retirement community setting is by its nature a social endeavor. Getting to know your fellow residents is another aspect of the process of settling in. Memorizing the names of everyone who lives with you may be an overwhelming thought and it is unrealistic to expect that of yourself. A common anxiety among people who share a living environment is the fear of not remembering someone's name. Many communities encourage all staff to wear their names and titles in a prominent place on their person. This helps you know to whom you are speaking, and if she or he is the right person to address your concerns. Some communities encourage everyone to wear a name badge to help fellow residents remember names.

Begin to make the acquaintance of people whom you see most often. Include, for example, your immediate neighbors, those persons with whom you share common interests, your dinner companions and those who seem attractive to you. As time goes by, you will naturally become acquainted with more people, but having a couple of contacts can be helpful as you start this process. Seeing a familiar face can help you feel more comfortable and can break the ice when you enter a new group.

You will probably find that your neighbors on your floor or wing of a floor form a small group. A resident reflected:

> We're sort of like a little community ourselves. And you grow so that, you know them more, and there are several that are more interesting than some of the other people. After dinner we sometimes stand in the hall and chat for some time.

Activities are a major way of discovering what you have in common with others. Make a point of attending those activities that are of greatest interest to you. You are more likely to meet others with similar interests. The activity itself can be a springboard for getting to know one another better and sharing other experiences.

Informal shared interests also will help you find acquaintances. For example, an active bridge party that rotates evening games in the apartments of the players is common in many communities. In our study many residents spoke with warmth and enthusiasm about their new friends. They described their general impression as congenial. They could choose their own level of social involvement without pressure from others to participate, yet most felt welcomed to join in interactions, and could acquaint themselves with the others without feeling formal or awkward.

One woman stated:

> Best of all, I like Sarah, she is such a wonderful, kind, feeling person. We had a relationship immediately.

Another woman expressed her enjoyment of others:

> You know, you make friends and one thing leads to another. You have a lot of fun. Sometimes we all get to giggling down there in the dining room, and if you think it's noisy when they're just talking you should hear it when they're laughing.

If your community has the policy of open seating for meals it can form the mechanism for social mixing because you can select a different table and dining companions at each meal. The lobby outside the dining room is a gathering place as residents wait for the dining room to open. You will also find that many people stay after meals to socialize.

We have already mentioned and given an example of the problem of being a newcomer when there is assigned seating, or when some residents have claimed a special place as their own. If you inadvertently sit in someone else's seat, it can make you feel unwelcome and uncomfortable. This is how a woman expressed her feeling:

The worst experience that I had when I first came was finding a place to sit in the dining room. Seats are not assigned, but all the people in the old section were assigned at one time. And they are clannish, they get together and they sit together and if you sit in the seat, they say, that's so-and-so's seat, and you are brand new and don't know anyone. Now if I see anybody wandering around, I get up to help them find a place.

Remember, it takes just a simple question to ask if someone already has reserved a place, and it will save you embarrassment or feelings of rejection. Other seats will be open to you, and you will feel accepted by new people.

Forming Friendships

Finding a friend is a rare gift. You now have an excellent chance to meet new people with whom you share common interests and enjoyment. You will find that you will form deeper relationships with some and welcome them into the more intimate social circle generally reserved for friends and family. One of the greatest advantages of group living is the potential to meet new people with whom to share your experiences.

Friendships take time to form, and are as unique as the people who are friends. Many people who move into a group setting find that they have had similar life experiences and face similar challenges, forming the basis of a friendship. You will find people with whom you have common interests or a shared history, and with whom you want to share companionship, support or exchange of talents and resources. Not feeling lonely is among the most positive aspects of communal life.

Romance

The possibility of romance is present in situations where people meet day after day and share common interests. As humans, we seek companionship and intimacy. Recent losses may hone feelings of loneliness, leading to a desire to share one's intimate life with another. Spouses who have devoted many years to the care of their loved ones who have since died may welcome the opportunity to recapture a healthy, active romantic life. For a single person, a retirement community offers the chance to meet many prospective partners. It may surprise you to have concern again about the rules of the dating game, especially if it has been years since engaging in this type of activity. Most members of retirement communities have witnessed marriages among residents who have discovered love and companionship in new friendships. Life is full of wonderful opportunities, and this may be one of them.

Romance, by definition, is a mutual feeling of attraction and regard for another person. Unwanted advances, however, are not pleasurable. It is your right to set the limits of your relationships and establish boundaries that make you feel comfortable. As friendships form, they may progress to more intimate levels. Sometimes the two parties do not share the same perception of the desired level of intimacy. It is here that communication can clarify the level at which you feel at ease. If you experience unwelcome overtures and are not comfortable letting the person know how you feel, you may elicit the assistance of the administration who want to ensure the safety and well-being of all members of the community.

Fitting in is a process that results in a feeling of interpersonal warmth and congeniality. Achieving social integration in your new setting will help you feel at home. You will be an important addition to the community, and will give your special interests and talents to the group.

In the next chapter we will consider your family relationships, and how you can help your adult children adjust to your life transition.

CHAPTER 10

Dealing With Your Children

Caregiving is one of the most common experiences of adult children and older adults. Family members provide support and care to one another in many different ways. They lend an ear when a loved one has troubles; they provide shelter, meals and may help with personal care.

Children often feel guilty about elderly parents. Role reversal may be taking place in which your children begin to take on a caregiving role, in ways you once parented them. It is not uncommon for children to assume that their parents have diminishing capabilities and are unable to make the decisions that most affect their lives. They listen to their friend's stories and worry that their parents may slip and fall, not take medications on time or become increasingly isolated. Sometimes they report worrying about their parents and are unable to sleep at night because they are concerned something will happen to them. You don't want to cause undue worry to your children either. However, it is important that you assess whether their worries are warranted.

Finding Common Goals

You share with your children the goal of avoiding preventable mishaps. That is what this book is all about. Your change of housing may put aside the greatest worry that you will be alone if something happens to you. Whereas you shouldn't move because it will put your children's minds at ease, you do need to plan realistically and avoid crisis decision-making. At this point, you can take the active role in deciding your future. This is what one person had to say about her mother:

> Every time I bring up the subject of her future, my mother just sits there in stony silence glowering at me. All I want is to open up the conversation and talk with her about her future. She's all alone and what if she falls at night? It would be morning before anyone even knew about it. She has friends, but they don't call all the time. I have tried the guilt-trip approach, telling her that I worry about her. She tells me that now I know how she felt when I was late getting home as a teenager. But I just don't know what to do, and we always end up ruining our visit together because of this argument.

Sometimes circumstances accelerate the moving process, as with this woman whose family completed her move while she was hospitalized with a fractured hip:

> As far as my family's concerned, I don't want to draw any judgments on my son because I don't think he would have done it without feeling. They wanted to clear the house and get it rented and get me placed. And, I couldn't face some decisions, so he was in a rather difficult position in some ways, too. I just wish he had let me be involved as much as I could have been.

Deciding the type of assistance or care you may need is complex and changes over time. Different perceptions of the problems and potential solutions may further complicate the matter. Adult children have stereotypes of what it means to grow old, their feelings of wanting to be protective and helpful, and their own interests as they try to balance the demands of their own families with the assistance they would like to provide to you.

During times of family crisis, old wounds may be opened. Keep in mind that you may be trying to meet their needs, not yours. Try to understand the source of their concern. How has your family dealt with conflict before? Do you share similar values and perceptions? How well do you communicate with one another? There are difficult decisions to face in later life, and the alternatives arouse mixed feelings. Sometimes the effort of working as a family to define the problem, examine different viewpoints and generate potential solutions can be worthwhile. This provides the opportunity to discuss assumptions and values openly where they can be considered and understood by all involved. You can guide the process by explaining your rationale for the move, how you have planned for it and by communicating your priorities to your children. If it is important for you to make the decision on your own, let them know in what ways you welcome their involvement. The process is as new to them as it is to you, and you can help the whole family come through the experience with positive feelings.

There are many ways to make decisions, and you will be unique in how you make yours. Decisiveness can be its own reward, as this woman who made her move while her daughter was on vacation recalls:

> I called my daughter in Las Vegas and I told her. And she said, "What?" And I said, "Yes, you won't stumble over me when you get home." And she said, "Well, if that's what you want." And I said, "I'm very satisfied, I've only been here a couple of days, but I kind of fit right in." So she's real happy for me now.

Avoiding Overprotection

You can set the tone for the relationship and establish the ground rules for how you will resolve issues that concern you. Don't protect your children from your own problems because it is likely that they want to know about you. Continue to share your personal worries, but make it clear that they are your worries, not theirs. Stress that you want to talk about things, but don't feel you need constant advice. Assure them that you are competent to make your own decisions, and seek their advice on areas in which you feel you need help. Also focus on the professional assistance you are receiving.

Adult children sometimes try to protect elderly parents. Knowing that you have problems of your own, they may avoid confiding theirs to you. One man said this:

> I was truly dismayed to find out from someone else that my daughter was getting a divorce. I had an idea that she had some personal problems, but she always put on a happy face for me when she came visiting from another state. On the telephone she always chatted about the minor details of her life, what the grandchildren were doing and things like that. She sounded okay and I didn't worry about her. Then when I found out about her divorce, I was awfully hurt. When I confronted her with this knowledge she said she didn't want to worry me. Why? Just because I'm old?

Showing an interest in the lives of your children and focusing on their concerns as well as yours can bring balance to the relationship—you can both provide and receive support from each other. Reciprocity is an important feature of our relationships, as described by this woman:

> I am busy and my children are busy, I don't expect them to jump for me anytime I holler. I know I can rely on them, they are always there when I need them. I just don't bother them and I don't get upset when they are busy.

They also don't get offended when I am too busy to go with them. They call on me for help, too. My granddaughter drops her baby off when she goes shopping and I take care of him, he's such a cutie.

Keeping Them Busy Helping You

Think about what will really help you as you make your decision to move, as you decide where to go, and during your move and settling in phases. Consider the particular strengths of family members and how they can be most effective. Then ask your children for assistance, by outlining what you would find most helpful and by defining the scope of their involvement. Keep them busy doing what you want them to do to avoid meddling where you don't want it.

Conducting the preliminary evaluation of housing alternatives can involve considerable travel and effort. It may be beneficial to you if your children did the beginning survey of available options, narrowing the choices down to the leading three or four. One woman found this most helpful:

> So my kids passed by here and went in, and they called me, "Mother, I think we found a place for you." I could not walk too easily, and I was half desperate. So I came here to visit and decided it was the place for me. They really made it easier on me.

A good way your children can help you, particularly if they live nearby, is to provide an escape hatch for you if you decide to move into a retirement community. Work out a backup plan with them in case your move proves to be more stressful to you or you feel you have made a mistake. For example, if they can help you keep your home intact for a short time you may feel better about your move, particularly if you have serious misgivings about it. A grandchild or other relative or friend of a relative may be willing to house sit in your home for a brief time. This is particularly important if you decide not to sell your home right away. This is what a man said:

> I was so grateful that my granddaughter and her husband were willing to store some of my things for a while. I just couldn't bring myself to give it all away at once. This came about because I asked them if they would be willing to help me. It also helped to get them to realize that I was able to make my own decisions as a responsible adult, not a doddering old fool.

Asking for What You Need and Want

Unless you want your closets and drawers to become cluttered again, tell your children what you would really like to receive for birthdays and holidays. Keep in mind that some useful gifts are those that are difficult for you to get for yourself. Ask for taxi vouchers, boxes of assorted greeting cards with stamps and other things you can use. A prepaid telephone card will help you stay in touch with friends and family and comes in many dollar amounts. If they can afford it, a cordless telephone can be a blessing for people who have difficulty getting to the telephone quickly. An answering machine is of great assistance in not missing calls or screening calls before you pick up the telephone. Don't be shy about asking for things you would like to have. Your children will be grateful to know what to get you. After all, how much more bath oil can you use?

The most valued gifts are those of time and effort. Asking your child to go with you as you assess housing communities and being there to help you in the decision-making process will be as fulfilling to your child as it is to you. You have probably shared a great deal together in the past; now is the time to share your future as well. As you get settled you may need help in hanging your pictures or rearranging your drawers. Instead of having your children make the decision for you, speak up and ask for what will help you.

Letting Them Be Supportive

Support means letting your children know that they can still count on you, even though you may be negotiating new boundaries of support and freedom. Wherever you choose to move, make it clear that you want to remain a vital part of their lives. A man said this:

> My daughter always asked my advice about financial matters, and then when I moved to the senior community suddenly she stopped asking my advice. It was sort of like I had gone on a shelf. Finally, I had to tell her that while I had lost my ability to navigate without a cane, my brain was still in operation. She laughed and told me she was

glad I had brought it up because she hadn't wanted to burden me with doing her income tax that year. I laughed and told her I loved doing it and to send it along.

Family Dynamics

Practice open communication by making your needs and wants clear, particularly concerning your finances and health. Broaching difficult problems requires sensitivity by both you and your children. Advance directives, the durable power of attorney for health matters and the living will, are important documents that ensure that others know what you want and will respect your wishes. Decide who to designate the durable power of attorney for health matters and be certain that all of your children understand that decision and the contents of your advance directives. In the words of one woman:

> I decided that I had to figure out which of my kids should hold the durable power of attorney for health matters and which should take care of my finances if I become incapacitated. I know my kids well, having raised them. My daughter is such a bubble-head, she couldn't balance her own checkbook. So I asked my son to take care of the finances if the need arose. I was convinced they would both go to pieces if the serious decision about whether I should go on life support had to be made, so I asked my nephew if he was willing to follow my wishes to the letter, and he was. Then I called a family meeting and just told them my decision. I didn't apologize, I didn't waver, I just told them right out. And I can't tell you how good it felt. I was in control and I might have spared them a lot of grief.

Helping Them Let Go

Don't let your children hover over you acting like you are helpless. Be firm in letting them know that you have your life in order, and that you are making new friends. Introduce them to your friends and neighbors to reassure them that you can make it on your own without their constant help. Your getting old is a new experience for your children too. They may even feel resentful that you are aging and that they will one day have to do without you. You can help them cope with the changes in your lives by keeping the channels of communication open.

As we reach the final chapter in this book, we turn again to the issues involved in transitions with a focus on new beginnings. In our last chapter, we hope we will help you put the entire experience into perspective and promote finding the satisfaction and peace you want in your new home.

CHAPTER 11

Reconciling Changes

There is more to settling into your new home than just figuring out how to go about your daily routines and sorting out your possessions. A part of settling in is the private and personal process of reconciling the life changes you have recently experienced. This process occurs throughout life as personal situations change; yet in the face of change, it is essential to seek continuity and a sense of identity.

There is considerable variation among people for the disruption a move to a retirement community causes. Some people report no significant interference in their lives and perceptions, while others experience many different changes that challenge their views of themselves and require considerable personal adjustment. Reconciling these life changes includes recognizing the changes, creating new views of yourself because of them, and accepting the new situation.

Recognizing Changes

The degree of life disruption experienced by people who move varies according to the kinds of precipitating circumstances, the ways the move unfolds and personal responses. Frequently, changes begin to take place before the move and may be factors in the decision to move. Change entails personal losses, including loss of space, mobility, former homes and possessions.

Apartment living may require letting go of opportunities such as gardening or entertaining guests. A woman tells her story:

> My sister and her husband would visit about once a month and instead of driving home they used to stay in my spare room, they always used to have it and they had a lot of stuff in it, just made it real easy. Now I'm not sure what's going to work. My brother-in-law doesn't feel comfortable here like he did in the other place. I was sort of sorry that he would feel that way and yet it was amusing in a way too cause I feel the same way.

Moving to smaller quarters in a retirement community may change the roles you play in your family circle. If you have traditionally hosted large family gatherings and welcomed overnight guests, you may find that your son, daughter or other family member will now take on this activity. If you have a kitchen in your new home you may still want to contribute your specialties to family gatherings. Find an acceptable compromise so that you can continue to contribute and feel involved in these activities.

Concurrent with the move, many people give up driving. It is difficult to anticipate the extent of change that the loss of personal transportation may impose, by limiting freedom of movement and opportunity to leave the community. This can restrict your activities to the immediate vicinity of your community and to those areas reached via formal arrangements through the facility or family and friends.

Loss of physical mobility may also be a significant life change. Because the new environment is easier on you (with little house-keeping, yard work and climbing up and down stairs) there may be a tendency to become more sedentary. Although the demands of your former home may have become excessive, you may miss the exercise of walking up and down stairs or mowing the lawn. Unless you find a way to continue regular exercise or physical activity, you may find that you become subject to lack of energy, lethargy and a loss of motivation to be more active.

A final source of personal loss may involve mourning for your former home and significant possessions. If you had the opportunity and time to prepare for the move and distribute valued possessions to people who would treasure them, you are more likely to accept the loss of certain belongings. Possession losses are most acutely felt by those who have little participation in the decision to move and the process of sorting and distributing belongings.

A second major source of change for many people is the social environment. Most of us have not lived in close physical proximity with so many other people, except during school or college days. In delivering services to many people as efficiently and economically as possible, communities organize meals and other services with a set schedule. This regimentation, particularly at meal times, may impose an unaccustomed structure to your life. On the other hand, you may appreciate and feel secure with the routines the community offers you and look forward to the set times for your meals and conversations with other people.

The characteristics of fellow residents are an important aspect of the social environment. There will be some with mental or physical impairment and you may not welcome the daily reminders of the frailties of old age. A great challenge for people who live in retirement communities is figuring out how to get along together. This means finding people whose company you enjoy, and limiting your exposure to those with whom you do not want to spend a great deal of time.

You may find that your social changes extend beyond your new home to your broader social network. It is common to have less contact with your former neighbors and friends, especially if the move is more than a few miles from your previous neighborhood. Often, there is less opportunity to get together with family and old friends because of difficulty driving or getting around.

One sad aspect of aging is having friends and family members die. You may find that your long-standing friendships are becoming fewer as you become a survivor of your group of friends. One woman we interviewed stated:

I had made a lot of friends in Seattle, and I had neighbors. There's not a one of them alive. They're all dead or out of town in nursing homes of some kind. So there's nobody here and I am just really alone except for my family.

It is possible to remain in contact with friends and neighbors through involvement in outside activities. Friends may be providing you with some assistance, offering to do laundry, errands or providing a ride to your activities. Take them up on their offers so that you may remain in contact with these important people. You can find ways to reciprocate their favors by offering to contribute to the cost of gas, or providing some services such as sewing, letter writing or sharing other talents.

The amount of contact you have with your family may stay the same, or it may even increase when you move to your new home. Find out if you may have guests for meals, or whether there is a private dining area so that you may invite others for a meal. You can help your family adjust to your new living situation by sharing the routines with them, such as how to enter the community and sign in, if required, and your general schedule. Find ways to involve your family and friends in your new life. Perhaps you need to go shopping once a month and would like to have the opportunity for an outing of several hours. If you let your family know, they may welcome the opportunity to contribute.

Creating a New Self-Image

Moving may require some alterations in how you view yourself. Part of adjustment means creating a new, revised and positive image of yourself. This is not a new task but one that you have been experiencing all your life. Once all the fuss and activity associated with making the move are over, you will find time for contemplation and reflection. Now that you have done it, how do you feel? The experiences of others may be helpful to you in your own reflections.

Many people view the move to retirement communities as their last planned relocation. After going through the process, they have a feeling of great satisfaction in having put their affairs in order and tied up loose ends. The thought that they have taken care of so much leaves them with a sense of accomplishment and the knowledge they are not leaving unwieldy disorder for survivors to disentangle. A woman described the importance of clearing the way for the future:

> Older people know that you're on the way out, you can't help but be. And I thought well now if I go completely blind I better take care of things now, you know, getting rid of things so that we leave our children, what little we have, in good order and not an accumulation of just things for our family to take care of afterward. That's important too.

Another woman echoed this sentiment:

> Moving settled things. Like moving out, I knew that was
> going to be a tremendous thing, moving from that house.
> And I'm very thankful that I moved in here. It was a lot
> of relief. Thinking at least that is over with.

The move may be a way to take an active role in preparing for
decline and death. Most people, after reaching the age of 70 or 80,
have witnessed the last years of others. It is common to have a good
sense of what you want to do and what is important for the years to
come. Many people want to take care of business before health or
other limitations affect their ability to make choices and carry them
out independently. Moving to retirement communities can crystal-
lize many choices and make the future clear. Instead of feeling sadness following this process, many describe a sense of satisfaction
and greater self-esteem for a job well done.

A move hastens thoughts about the future. What now? Some
people recount a feeling of being in limbo, now that they have made
a major decision and their affairs are in order. You may find that you
are thinking about your remaining years, wondering what is to come
and how long you will live. You might be comparing your health
and age with the health and ages of close family members when
they died, including your parents and siblings. For the first time in
your life, you may be thinking about the limits of your life. A
woman reflects matter-of-factly on her death:

I don't have any heart trouble or blood pressure or anything like that so I can't determine what I'm going to die
of yet. That's a hard calculation, figuring how long I'm
going to be around. I just hope I'll stay well enough to die
in my bed but not to have to be there too long before I die.

Throughout your life, you have experienced both ups and
downs. Those who are successful in adjusting accept these fluctu-
ations and life changes and keep going. The changes associated
with your move may be occurring simultaneously with changes
you were already experiencing with age. Being in a setting where
the frailties of old age are more evident may pose a special challenge to you.

One man made the comment:

I make a joke that I came in healthy and became like the
other older people here. I don't feel as if I'm incapacitated to the extent many are. That was one of my objections
to coming, that I would be amongst older people who are
not nearly as alive and active as someone else. I'm not
sure yet that I am at the point where I am satisfied to be
associating only with people my age or older.

The following quotation highlights the discrepancy many feel
between inner feelings and the outward evidence of aging:

You know the trouble with an older person is, you don't
think old, you think young. You think you would like to
do some of the things that the young people are doing or

you do try to do things that the young people do. I keep thinking, all these old people in here and then I think, well, you're crazy, you're just as old, if not older than a lot of them are. I don't know how you get this fixation but you do, that you're still a kid. I'm beginning to feel the frailties of old age. It doesn't bother me that I'm going to die because I know it's time, but it gets kind of hard sometimes because it's hard on me to take care of my husband. It started to wear on me and that's when I began to age.

A positive benefit of aging is that many people feel more tolerant, are more willing to see multiple views and have a calmness that helps them cope with the social environment of retirement communities. With greater tolerance, you are more likely to accept the physical and mental impairments of other residents and extend help and support to others.

When you think about how you view yourself, what comes to mind? Do you reflect on your accomplishments, the major events in your life, your family, your personality, your current activities or your hopes and dreams? Our identities grow with us throughout our lives and shift with changing circumstances.

Your current self-image is probably a combination of elements from your past, present and what you think your future will be. You are a survivor, and you may have a well-deserved sense of pride in making it through drastic world changes and personal adversity. You may derive great satisfaction from your personal achievements and those of your family and dear friends. Your past affiliations and commitments may contribute to your sense of identity.

Your views of who you are now may not be as clear. An upheaval such as a move and the resulting circumstances may erode a strong sense of self, leaving you sure about who you are not, but not too clear about who you are. With so many people of similar age, it is easy to make comparisons with others, identifying qualities that you are certain you don't have and do not wish to have.

Particularly in the midst of personal change, it is comforting to note the problems that others have. While this may be a source of solace, it does not contribute to strengthening your own identity. As you continue to adjust to your recent changes, your personal growth and ability to develop and maintain significant roles and relationships form the foundation for a stronger sense of self.

It is difficult for anyone to face the future with certainty. During this period in your life, you may be even more hesitant to make too many plans because of doubt about your future health and abilities. You have just experienced a unique opportunity to tie up loose ends and resolve personal matters, leaving your future clear of some encumbrances of daily life. Because of the limited ability to improve your assets and income, and your uncertainty about your future needs, you may have concerns about your financial resources for the future. You may be the kind of person who believes that tomorrow will take care of itself, or you may be worrying about your future. If you have made your plans carefully, you have placed yourself in the best possible position to face the future with all of its uncertainties.

Viewing Moving as a Part of Life

As with all life transitions, remember that new beginnings follow endings. We have discussed in some detail the losses and changes associated with the move. These represent many endings of your previous situation. Now that you have moved, you have the wonderful opportunity to make a new beginning and create a positive phase in your life. You are in a new circumstance and you have the chance to try out novel ways of being and approaches to situations. Now is the time to remember why you wanted to make the move in the first place. However attractive your old situation may seem in retrospect, there were important reasons for thinking about making a change. It is likely that as time went on, many more reasons to move would have evolved.

So, how does one adjust? Research suggests that those who make the effort to become involved in their new community and see their experiences in a positive way adjust better. It may sound trite, but attitude has a great deal to do with it.

There is evidence that people who hold optimistic views of themselves and the world live longer and healthier than those who see the world negatively. Are you the type of person who finds the positive in any situation? Or are you someone who becomes overwhelmed by the negative aspects and has difficulty seeing the benefits before you? If you are the first kind of person, chances are very good that you will adjust rapidly and smoothly.

If you can consider your current experience in the context of your broader life experience, you are probably going to adapt well. While present circumstances may seem less than the best, it may be helpful to reflect on other times you have felt down—did you get through that experience, did you find that pretty soon, something good came along to balance out the difficulties? It is the ability to take the good with the bad, and recognize that the present situation is limited and does not reflect your total life, that will help you get through.

Part of this process is developing a full and meaningful life for yourself now. It is comforting and helpful to think about good times in the past, but the challenge is to create positive times in the present. Dwelling on your concerns for the future is less productive. If you have made careful plans, there is not much else you can do to influence what is to come. You can adjust to your present situation best through finding ways to make the most of your life.

Developing a Sense of Self

There are many ways to develop a strong sense of self. One is to get to know and get involved with other people in your residence and in the greater community. We all have different levels of desire for social engagement and it is possible for you to seek out just the amount with which you are comfortable. Start with close neighbors or people who seem interesting to you. The hardest part is the first introduction; from there the relationship will progress more easily.

If you are uncomfortable initiating contact with someone, make sure you are in public places and can observe the comings and goings of the community. Chances are you will get to know who's who and before long you will be more comfortable.

Another way to develop a stronger sense of self is to cultivate a meaningful task in your social circle or the community. All of us play many roles in our lives, some formal and some informal. Within a community, there are opportunities to embrace assignments that will be recognized by others. These may include membership on a committee or the Resident Council, appointment as a safety officer on your floor, a confidante, a driver (if you have a car), a member of the craft group or a social organizer. If you have a particular ability, think about how you could apply that interest to community life. There are benefits as you get the chance to do something that you enjoy and you meet others with similar interests. It doesn't take long for other residents to recognize the role you play in the community. This recognition can go a long way to generate a sense of worth and belonging.

Find a way of expressing your talents and interests in the current setting. It is easier to reconcile your life changes if you can find an outlet for self-expression. For example, one woman we interviewed had been a missionary and her congregation had always asked for her advice. In her new community, she became the leader of the Bible study class and continued to counsel other residents and pray with them in times of distress. Although she reported feeling over-burdened by the ills of others at times, clearly she derived considerable satisfaction from her contributions to the life of the community. A man who enjoyed singing organized the community's amateur musicians for a weekly sing-along.

Those who are unable to find expression for their interests are most likely to view their present existence as a time of being in limbo lacking personal meaning. One man had always been active outdoors until recent health problems accelerated the move. He discussed his lack of ability to express his interests:

> I was always a farmer, I've always had a plot of ground I could dig in and now we don't. I tried to assist the gal who does the garden work here and she said she didn't desire or want any help so I wouldn't help her now. I don't know what the word is to use but . . . it isn't as enjoyable as it used to be. No, it's pretty much a drag.

A final strategy in developing a strong sense of self is to concentrate on the advantages of your new situation and minimize the losses. For the first time since childhood, you may have freedom from certain responsibilities. Think about ways to use that extra time and energy for yourself. You deserve it. Enjoy not feeling dependent on friends and family for some of your activities of daily living and take full advantage of the services and amenities that you have chosen.

Accepting the Current Situation

We found that most of the people who moved to retirement communities expressed satisfaction with their choices. Many conveyed surprise and pleasure that their move had gone so smoothly. It commonly takes a few weeks to a few months to become settled. At the end of this phase, most feel relatively content. With some exceptions, most people accept their current circumstances and recognize that certain sacrifices were necessary for a greater good. A woman reflected on her acceptance:

> It took me three months to adjust. Three months I was worse than ever, it depressed me so much. But now, I thought I would make the best out of it. I thought I would never get used to it. But I managed. If I say I am happy, this is not true, but I made up my mind I can live here.

Others are delighted with the new opportunities and their freedom from the demands of maintaining a home. Another woman shared her excitement:

> It's wonderful right now, this is the time to be thinking about it. I have the time to do the things I want to do. I really get a thrill out of music and I was always running too fast to sit down and enjoy it. I was always busy, because there was always something out there that you had to do. But now there's so much time.

After several months, a few people continue to be unhappy and discontented with their living situation. These people are unable to reconcile the changes in their lives and remain dissatisfied with their current life experience. There may be other problems beyond the move itself, such as health or problems with mobility that increase the difficulty with acceptance. If you are still having difficulty accepting the change of residence 9 to 12 months after the move, it is possible that the situation is not the right one for you. If this is the case, it may be time to explore other housing options to see if you can find a better fit for your needs and desires.

Trusting Yourself

You are the expert. You know yourself better than anyone else does and you have survived many different circumstances in your life up to this point. It is important to maintain your confidence and remember how you got through other hard times in your life. Remember that moving and settling in is a process that occurs over an extended time. Give yourself the chance to take your time to get through it.

How Do I Know if I Have Adjusted?

Although everyone experiences some upheaval in their physical and social environment with a move into retirement communities, there are differences in perceptions of the types of difficulties encountered and the personal significance of the disruption. Adjustment to retirement communities occurs at many levels. Over the course of the move, you adjust to both the small and large changes you face. You may have faced multiple transitions, including changes in health, mobility and social situation, all superimposed over the moving transition. Not only were you adjusting to the move, but also to other changes that were interwoven and inter-related to your move.

You may get a general sense of your adjustment by considering how you feel about your life right now. Are you satisfied? Do you feel a sense of well-being? Or are you sad or blue? These feelings are a reflection of your general sense of how things are going and may or may not be related to your current living situation. If you are feeling satisfied and mostly pleased, chances are that you have adjusted to the general circumstances of your life.

If you are dissatisfied with your life and you feel blue most of the time, it may be helpful to think about which things are bother-ing you. You may be facing a set of circumstances that are over-whelming, or you may be missing the support you need from peo-ple who care about you or you may be feeling somewhat hopeless. In thinking about the issues that are most bothersome, consider whether they are general problems that would be occurring no mat-ter where you live or whether the problems relate to your new liv-ing situation. If you conclude that your new living situation is part of your problem or is making other problems worse, it may not be the best place for you at this time. You may find it helpful to seek the advice and support of a friend or professional to help with your problems adjusting. You may be comfortable talking with your spir-itual advisor, counselor, therapist, nurse, social worker, psycholo-gist, psychiatrist or another health professional. A few sessions will help you gain perspective and make a positive plan.

Your adjustment to your new community is a part of your general adjustment, and you will know how well you have done by how much you feel at home. Do you have a sense of warmth and belonging? Are you physically comfortable? Have you invested time and energy in your apartment? Does your new home offer you the freedom to be yourself? If you answered "yes" to these questions, chances are very good that you have settled into your new home successfully. If you have adjusted well, you feel at ease in the environment socially, physically and emotionally.

People who have successfully adjusted to the move and the surrounding events usually regard the reasons for the move as legitimate, were involved in the decision making and planning phases of the moving process, have allowed themselves to create new homes that express their identities and provide comfort, and they are involved socially. The following quotation by a woman illustrates her adjustment.

> We're comfortable here. They really are a nice bunch of
> people here. You almost have to challenge your life in the
> channels that you've got. I've had lots of things happen in
> our lives, but if you brooded or yelled and cried about it
> all these years you'd never get above it. So it's been a
> great life and everything, it always turns out for the best.
> It might be hard in doing it, but then it does happen.

It is possible that the choice to move to a retirement community was not the best decision for you. You may generally feel good about your life now. The circumstance on which you made the decision to move may have changed. This was the experience of a man who had moved following the death of his wife, looking for assistance and support. As he worked through his grief and began to extend himself again, he recognized the limitations of the current setting. His words follow:

> I came here because I was interested in a place that didn't put many demands on me. I was real mordant and unhappy after my wife died. And then I started the recovery in the last six months. I enjoy life. Not as much as I used to, but I'm beginning to snap out of it. My adjustment took a while. I'm the youngest person here, by about five years. And the petty squabbles they get into and the imagined or actual slights and insults that are exchanged. And the people going around in walkers, well I'm not ready for that. So finally, I decided to move out. This is not the place for me.

Adjustment is not a simple process, but it is a tremendous accomplishment when done successfully. In thinking about your life change, consider both your general outlook and your contentment in your new home. If you have concerns, take advantage of the people who are willing and able to help. The staff of the retirement community is often helpful and can help you work through some transitional difficulties.

Other resources in the community may also be of assistance. Don't forget that you have been successful until now, or you wouldn't be thinking about these issues. Take the time to recognize the achievements of the last months in executing such a major decision. While we have little control over the challenges that arise during our lives, we can make a difference in how we cope with the changes. We wish you the best in the transitions you face.

CHAPTER 12

Staying Healthy in Your New Setting

If you were given the chance to design your own future, there is no doubt that you would prefer to stay in good health and keep a normal level of activity throughout your life regardless of how old you live to be. Although you have to accept some minor inconveniences and adjustments as you get older, such as having to change eyeglasses periodically, getting a hearing aid, or accepting minor aches and pains, it is the worry and the fear of becoming seriously ill or incapacitated that frightens most of us. You have to maintain good health to enjoy your relationships with family and friends and to keep doing what you enjoy the most.

The principles of aging successfully are well accepted. Aim to prevent diseases that make you age faster. Stay in control of your life by making your personal choices clear. Exercise your mind and your body to promote the best function possible. Preserve vitality through independence and self-confidence.

Healthy lifestyles are critical to maintaining good health and slowing the effects of aging. Researchers are finding a higher degree of functional ability is maintained later in life than previously thought. This reassuring finding is due to the fact that the reserve capacity for most functions is so large that no measurable fall in function, for example of intelligence or memory, occurs until late in life, and then only among those who suffer disease. Most importantly, lifestyle changes have a much larger impact on health and aging than previously understood.

New findings in gerontology emphasize that our health behaviors go a long way to retain and enhance function in later life. There are three key behaviors or characteristics important to achieve the goal of aging successfully:

- Low risk of disease and disease-related disability
- High mental and physical function
- Active engagement with life

Today we know that many infirmities that used to be considered "just part of aging" aren't normal aging but are due to various illnesses. Mountains of research show that unremarkable factors well known to everyone are key to physical and mental well-being. The secrets of long-lived people who have maintained their health and energy provide essential advice because it is never too late to start living a healthier life. These important factors are:

- Maintain regular physical activity
- Eat a healthy diet
- Avoid smoking

- Use moderation in drinking alcohol or taking drugs

- Work with your health provider

- Maintain important connections with others

- Keep your mind active and have a positive mental attitude

Regular Physical Activity

The importance of regular physical activity cannot be over-stated. In their comprehensive book *Successful Aging*, Drs. John Rowe and Robert Kahn state that the simple, basic fact about exercise and health is that fitness cuts your risk of dying. It doesn't get much more basic than that! They group couch potatoes with cigarette smokers as taking their lives into their own hands. Lack of physical activity, not aging, causes much of the decline in physical function associated with getting older. Exercise is like a wonder drug because it helps to relieve stress, helps curb the appetite, aids in alertness, relieves stiffness, and helps promote restful sleep. Physical activity, particularly weight bearing activities, increases strength and muscle size. It also adds to bone strength limiting the risk of osteoporosis and fractures, particularly of the hip, spine, and wrist. It helps to improve balance, thereby decreasing the risk of falling.

The recommendation is for regular physical activity for at least half an hour per day, most days of the week. If you choose walking as your exercise, to reap the benefits all you have to do is walk for half an hour most days of the week. Alternatives include using a stationary bicycle, dancing, aerobics classes, heavy gardening or housework, or swimming. You not only need to get in shape but you must stay in shape. The good news is that you don't have to work harder and harder to stay in the same shape; you just have to continue the level of training on a regular basis. In other words, use it or lose it.

Weight training helps muscles grow in size and strength, even for frail people of advanced age. Most retirement communities have an exercise room with equipment that you can use after you have discussed a plan with your health provider. Many offer classes for aerobic activities modified for older adults, such as calisthenics, dancing, yoga, and Tai Chi that will strengthen and relax you. It's much more fun to do it with the company of others and making a commitment to continue exercising on a regular basis will also help motivate you.

Walking outdoors is particularly pleasurable, but remember to shield yourself from the sun's rays. There is increasing evidence that unprotected eyes, as well as skin, suffer from the prolonged effects of the sun, so wear glasses with sufficient tint to screen out harmful sunlight and UVB radiation, and wear a sunscreen lotion with a Sun Protective Formula (SPF) of at least 15. A broad-brimmed hat or cap helps protect both your eyes and your skin.

A word of caution is indicated because there are risks with exercise. Minor muscular/skeletal injuries are fairly common and include such things as pulled muscles or torn ligaments. Before you embark on a new program of exercise, talk over what you plan to do with your health provider particularly if you are being treated for any chronic condition, such as heart or lung problems, and work with a qualified trainer or physical therapist.

The most common cause of injury in exercising is doing it aggressively too soon. Start out gradually and increase the time and intensity progressively. A well-rounded exercise program should always consist of a warm-up period to prevent injuring muscles. Limber them up before serious exercise, and allow for a cool down period for muscle recovery following the exercise.

If you skip exercising for a day or two, don't get discouraged. Just get back into your routine as soon as you can. If the activity you've chosen is too strenuous or causes injuries, slow down or switch to something else. As a general rule, if you can keep up your exercise program for the first month, it will most likely become a regular habit that you will look forward to and enjoy.

Eat a Healthy Diet

Although the same general nutritional guidelines for older adults as for those younger make sense, there are some specific age-related recommendations for healthy older persons. Nutritional requirements do change over time. Because aging men and women progressively lose muscle mass, it takes fewer calories to function normally. The basal metabolic rate (the energy used to perform basic body functions) drops by about 10 percent by the age of 75 years. Furthermore, because older persons are generally less physically active, the result is a substantial decline in caloric needs. To maintain your normal weight you have either to eat less or exercise more.

Water balance is an important aspect of overall nutrition. Dehydration is potentially serious, and older persons are at high risk because there is a decreased capacity to conserve water through the kidneys, and a significantly lower sensation of thirst. This is particularly troublesome combined with any infectious disease, for example, even the common cold. Older persons should consume about one and a half quarts of fluid daily. This doesn't have to be all water; fruit juices and other beverages can be taken as well. It takes effort to remember to drink fluids often, but the results are worth it. Fluids can aid in preventing constipation also.

If you live in a retirement community your meals will be balanced and nutritious, but since you choose what you will eat, remember that you need a balance of fats, carbohydrates and protein. Older people actually require more protein than do younger people. Protein insufficiency may reduce the ability to fight disease and heal wounds, and it may cut your overall muscle strength.

The goal of a healthy diet is to eat a wide range of foods every day from each of the major food groups: the bread, cereal, rice and pasta group; at least five helpings from the vegetable and fruit group (because fruits and vegetables of different colors indicate their mineral content it is desirable and attractive to mix a variety of them); the milk, yogurt and cheese group; and the meat, fish, beans, eggs and nuts group. If you find that milk and milk products are difficult for you to digest, be sure you tell your health advisor so that modification in your diet can be made. Foods high in fiber (beans and grains, vegetables, and fruits) are important in the diet. This indigestible residue passes through the bowel and attracts water, thus providing bulk to the stool so that it can pass easily.

The issue of supplemental vitamins is another factor you should discuss with your health advisor. Free radicals, the result of normal oxygen metabolism, are considered a major enemy in the aging process because they cause damage to cells throughout the body. Research is underway on the effects of antioxidant vitamins C and E on the body.

Herbal remedies have increased in number and many believe they help maintain or restore normal functioning, although some of the claims have not been substantiated through scientific research as yet. If you choose to practice what is commonly called "alternative or complementary medicine" be certain that you tell your health provider what you are taking. This is essential if you are taking any medications because the herbal substance may interfere with or augment the action of certain drugs.

One mineral of undisputed importance is calcium. Osteoporosis is a major health problem, particularly for older women, but men are not immune from this crippling disease of the bones. Adequate intake of calcium is difficult to achieve through diet alone; hence, most health providers recommend daily supplemental calcium with vitamin D, which is needed for its absorption. If you are at risk for osteoporosis because you are small boned, belong to a specific ethnic group (those of Asian and northern European ancestry are particularly vulnerable) or if other members of your family have suffered from it, you definitely should discuss prevention, which may include hormonal therapy, with your health provider.

Avoid Smoking

Smoking is implicated in all of the major causes of death of older adults in the U.S. and there is voluminous evidence that smoking shortens the life span. Furthermore, smoking-related diseases, such as cancer, emphysema, and stroke are particularly incapacitating. Smoking is also implicated in osteoporosis.

Nicotine is among the world's most addictive drugs. Although it is best to have never smoked, it is never too late to stop. It isn't easy to stop smoking, and many require some help. There are successful smoking cessation programs, and the American Cancer Society, the American Lung Association, your health provider or senior center will be able to refer you to one. Some people require physiological support through nicotine gum or patches. Some smokers choose to start cutting back on tobacco gradually, and set a date for quitting completely. Some can do it cold turkey. Quitting with a partner is sometimes helpful because you support and keep each other from setbacks.

Once you have quit smoking, there are a few tricks that former smokers have shared. They include keeping low-calorie snacks, sugarless gum, or toothpicks on hand, switching to drinking tea if you associate coffee with having a cigarette, and always sitting in a no smoking area in a public place. Regardless of how you choose to quit smoking, remember that although it isn't easy the rewards are many. Above all, congratulate yourself often on stopping!

Alcohol and Other Drugs

Although some research shows that a drink or two a day can help ward off heart disease and other ailments, aid digestion, and relieve stress, most health professionals say that if you don't drink now, don't start. An ounce or two of alcohol can have a greater impact on you as you get older. It not only makes you feel "woozier," which can lead to balance and falling problems, but it can aggravate other conditions. Moreover, older people who have never had a drinking problem when young can experience late-onset alcoholism in response to stressful events such as loss of a partner, family member or friends, poor health, retirement, or moving.

Alcohol abuse among older adults is a serious problem that needs prompt attention. Unfortunately, older problem drinkers tend to be overlooked by both health professionals and the general public due to their perceived low numbers. When retired it is easier to hide a drinking problem than when employed. Heavy drinkers have increased risk for illnesses, such as cirrhosis of the liver, obesity, high blood pressure, cancer, and accidents, both traffic related and in the home. Some heavy drinkers develop a form of dementia. Some have tremors or jerky movements. Alcohol is also thought to accelerate osteoporosis. Among older adults, the excessive use of alcohol leads to (or can be caused by) depression.

As you get older, the effects of both prescription and over-the-counter drugs will be changed. It is important to consult periodically with your health provider about appropriate dosage, which other drugs you are taking, and drug interactions with each other and with food. Be careful not to overuse over-the-counter drugs. Sleeping pills can become ineffective in combating insomnia and interfere with natural sleep and dream patterns. Gastrointestinal problems can be caused by the use of aspirin and nonsteroidal anti-inflammatory drugs commonly taken to alleviate muscle and joint aches and pains. This doesn't mean you should never take them; it means you should consult with your health advisor if you are taking any drug regularly.

Alcohol and drug dependence can be overcome; however, it is wisest to seek professional help to do so. Consult your health advisor, or contact the mental health department. The first essential step is to recognize that you have a problem. The second is to seek help.

Work with Your Health Provider

Although we have stressed the importance of taking charge of your own health through your lifestyle and habits, we also recommend that you seek periodic advice from your health professional, a physician or nurse practitioner familiar with the care of older adults. Even those with healthy lifestyles can have or develop ailments from hearing loss to heart disease with advancing age. Routine medical care can detect these problems, often early enough for successful treatment. There are many screenings today such as breast, pelvic, and pap smears for women and prostate examinations for men. Your blood pressure, your weight, and the intraocular pressure in your eyes should receive special attention. You should test your stool for hidden blood each year through a simple and inexpensive test. Routine analysis of your blood and urine should be done to determine the functioning levels of vital organs. Your primary health professional will assess risk factors because of your family history, lifestyle, ethnicity, and other factors. Based on these, a determination can be made about the schedule of screening tests needed.

Keeping current with your immunizations is essential. Although a thorough immunization plan is an important lifetime health investment that protects you against a host of life-threatening diseases, such as smallpox, diphtheria, and polio, it continues to be a very important part of your health as you get older. You will need to get a pneumococcal vaccine once, influenza vaccinations annually, and tetanus every 10 years. It is wise to become protected against hepatitis A and B as well. Protection against diseases that once were considered exotic and needed only for travel to less developed nations are now becoming problems because the world has shrunk with many visitors entering or citizens returning to our country daily bringing with them unwanted foreign microorganisms. Be sure you keep a record of your immunizations at home.

In working with your health professional, be assertive and informed. Describe your symptoms clearly and objectively. Provide a personal and family medical history and a list of all of the medications you are taking, both prescription and over-the-counter. Be honest about your health habits, both those that are positive and those that are not (such as smoking or excessive drinking). Remember, it's your health and your life so you fool only yourself if you don't talk about what is on your mind.

Choosing your health care provider is an important decision. You need to form a partnership so that you work together with the goal of meeting your health needs on your terms. You should seek one who is open and honest with you, who will answer your questions in a straightforward manner. Sharing the same values is important so that you can understand one another.

When you call to make your appointment be clear about why you want to see your health professional and how much time you think you will need. Come prepared by making a list of your questions and organize, and prioritize your needs so you can efficiently use the time. Ask what your symptoms might mean. If you don't understand medical terminology insist on explanations in words you understand. Repeat back what you have heard. Get a summary of your conversation, including technical terms that you can later look up. Keep records of your visits, what transpired, and what was said. Keep an account of your laboratory findings also. If you tend to forget what was said, either bring a tape recorder or a friend with you.

In your health care decision-making you need to get explanations about suggested options. It is important not to rush into any treatment, except in the case of an emergency. Ask what is needed and why. Find out about the benefits of any treatment or procedure and weigh that information against possible risks. Be certain that you understand exactly what is planned for you. If you feel insecure about asking questions, bring a trusted family member or friend to listen with you. Remember that only you can make the final decision, and then only after you have adequate information about the full range of available options.

The Mind-Body Connection

One aspect of cognitive ability that diminishes with age is a certain kind of memory, that which involves the intention to remember and the subsequent ability to recall a specific name, number, or location on demand. All older people find themselves racking their brains for a name or word that is well known to them, but which refuses to come to mind on demand. This reflects the reduction of explicit memory.

Other kinds of memory normally show little if any decline with age. When things previously seen or heard are presented again, older people recall and recognize them as well as those younger. Perhaps most important, something called working memory, the learned routines on which all of us rely in our daily lives, shows little decline with age.

However, older people do differ from younger people in the conditions they require for effective mental performance. Many younger people are able to do several tasks at once, such as listen to music or watch television at the same time as study for an upcoming examination. Older people do less well with distracting or competing conditions. The reason is quite clear: Older people are more distractible, less able to filter out stimuli that are irrelevant to the task at hand. It is important that older adults have the opportunity to focus on one project at a time.

Although most older adults misplaced keys and other personal items when they were younger, when it happens to them now they become quite fearful that they are losing their memory and headed toward one of the most feared conditions, Alzheimer's Disease (AD). The characteristics of AD are a progressive, sometimes insidious degenerative process that affects the brain and cognitive functioning. It is the most common of the dementias of older adults in our country. Although its symptoms include a gradual loss of memory, every time you can't remember someone's name it does not mean that you are headed for progressive disorientation of time and space. It is important to realize that Alzheimer's is not a consequence of normal aging; it has characteristic pathological features. Any significant changes in memory or mental function should be explored with one's health provider.

So how can we avoid or minimize cognitive decline? Many factors contribute to this desired outcome. Even genetic predestination does not tell us the whole story about mental functioning because dozens of studies pertaining to identical twins reared apart tell us that many factors are environmental and under our control. While the impact of genes on mental function is greater than some other characteristics, lifestyle measures to improve mental abilities are exceedingly strong.

Studies on successful aging found that people who are better educated, physically healthy and active, and have high self-esteem are most likely to maintain sharp mental abilities for a longer time in their lives. Research on centenarians indicates that they have maintained a vigorous interest in life and in activities that go beyond themselves. Belief in your own abilities to handle various situations has an impact on memory. This personality trait is known as "self-efficacy." Older people high in self-efficacy are more likely to view memory as a set of cognitive skills that can be learned and improved rather than being biologically determined and inevitably reduced by age.

There are exercises that can be done to improve memory; many are truly fun to practice. Games, particularly word games such as crossword puzzles and scrabble, and card games keep the mind working. Reading is another activity that helps improve intellectual functioning. Talking and arguing with others keep your brain active and occupied. Memory training (association, for example) can improve memory performance in older persons.

Possibly the most important factor in maintaining mental functioning in later years is social support. Experiments have indicated that persons who are given support and encouragement do better in tests of memory, playing of games (such as jigsaw puzzles), and other activities requiring mental functioning.

The Importance of Connection with Others

There can be no question that continuing close relationships with others – family and friends – is an important element in successful aging. Engagement and connection are vital to healthy aging and the absence of meaningful relationships poses a significant health threat. Our relationships fill many roles in our lives. They give us a sense of belonging, of being loved, and cared for. They give us affection, assistance, mutual obligation, trust, esteem, information. The most important aspect of connection is the meaning it has to you – that the type of support you get from others is the type you want and value. Important relationships may be with other living things as well – pets, or gardening – living things that depend on us.

Our relationships are our own responsibility – to form, to nurture, to challenge, to improve. Those who age most successfully are surrounded by a diverse network of friends and family, who represent different ages and different aspects of one's life. It sounds trite, but you have to be a friend to have a friend and we have to be prepared for changes in our primary relationships as we age, whether by death or illness or other reasons.

It is often easier to maintain and nurture an existing relationship than it is to start a new one. We can attend to our network and make it strong by reaching out to those who are important to us, being the first to initiate a resolution to a conflict, and by letting those close to us know that they matter. Family relationships, with siblings and other relatives can take on a new meaning with age, as those who share a common history with longstanding ties.

Contrary to many myths and stereotypes, older adults are sexual human beings, with persistent sexual desires, fantasies, and sexual expression to meet their needs. Older adults may need to adapt and change their sexual practices according to changing abilities or mobility. Previous interest, frequency, and enjoyment of sex in early life are reliable predictors of active sexuality in later years. A recent study showed that physically active persons between 40–80 years old were as active sexually as persons 20–40 years younger.

Sexual relations late in life often depend on the availability of a partner, with declines in activity being associated with death or illness rather than any other factor. With women living longer, this often has a greater impact on their ability to remain sexually active throughout life. Intimacy can be expressed in many ways, and touch, affection, caring for, and trusting another person are all important aspects of the relationship and for self-esteem.

Sexual dysfunctions, such as impotence, are not inevitable, but may be caused by systemic disorders (hypertension, diabetes), long-time interruption of activity, side effects of drugs, alcoholism, workaholism, excessive eating, or difficulties feeling desire for a long-time partner. Changes in physical appearance can have an effect on one's confidence or self-image. Concerns about sexual functioning should be discussed with your health care provider to explore reversible causes.

The Role of Emotions on Health

Positive emotions have constructive effects on the entire physical body while negative ones can hurt your physical health. For example, stress has been linked to headaches, higher blood pressure, and other symptoms. We know that the way you think about health changes it. Optimists even catch fewer colds. In addition to having better health habits, our emotions help our immune system to function better. There is evidence to suggest that optimists live longer than pessimists.

Optimism doesn't come easily; it takes a lot of practice. Here are some of the tricks: Every day count your blessings at least once, and more times if you are feeling cross and negative. Focus on the good rather than the bad. See that glass of water as half full, not half empty. It may sound like Pollyanna, but it really works. This doesn't mean that you shouldn't express anger or sadness when indicated; in fact, not expressing emotions may be detrimental to your health. But it isn't necessary to grow more pessimistic and cynical as you age. This is the behavior that leads to the stereotype that many older people are cranky and not much fun to have around. You can't do anything about getting older, so enjoy the years you have left and focus on the positive aspects of your life.

People who feel that they have control of events in their lives have better physical and psychological health than those who assume that nothing they do matters. Health professionals who work with individuals who have arthritis, for example, know that the self-management of symptoms is essential. To control problems, a variety of relaxation techniques and exercises can be learned with success. Your own actions make a difference, and you can learn to improve your health.

People use different strategies for coping with major life problems. Study after study has indicated that it is not necessarily the extent of the crisis that has occurred but the way that people cope with it that predicts the effect on health. There are negative ways to cope with a crisis. You can get angry, become bitter, drink heavily, or distort the facts. All of these ways are guaranteed to produce health problems. Or you can cope maturely by working to see the best in a given situation, anticipate better events that you are confident will come later, and use humor and altruism. By realizing that you have a choice in how you handle a problem you will maintain better health and minimize the detrimental effects.

Major changes or losses in your life can lead to depression, which can become a major problem. Be aware of the early symptoms of depression to seek treatment. These are loss of appetite, unintentional weight loss or gain, experiencing less interest in activities that previously were pleasurable, sleep disturbances, feelings of sadness, withdrawal, irritability, or anxiety, and fatigue. Mild depression may be alleviated by activities, such as exercise, talking with a friend, or a support group. Expect some depression to follow any loss, but if it continues for several months, seek professional assistance. If ever you should have thoughts of suicide, take this symptom very seriously and get immediate help through the emergency number of your health plan, or the nearest crisis center. Depression is treatable, particularly if it is recognized earlier rather than later.

As you get older it will be inevitable that you will lose some people who are dear to you – your partner, friends, neighbors.

Sadness and grief are an important part of the transition from one phase of life to another, and no one can tell another person how to grieve. There are generally recognized stages of grief that might help you deal with your emotions and those of others who are grieving. These are:

- Shock and denial: not being able to believe that the loss has occurred. After a death, the grieved person may behave as if the dead person is still alive and may see or hear that person.

- Anger: sometimes there is a need to point blame for the loss. Mourners may be angry with others for their loss, even if it isn't rational.

- Depression: feelings of being overwhelmed by the loss and experiencing some or all of the symptoms of depression.

- Reconciliation: realizing that life has to go on, and although the person lost is still missed, a return to normal life is possible.

As you get older your reaction to stress changes. Studies show that some older adults tend not to have a "fight or flight" reaction to stress, but rather a passive "freeze" reaction to it. Inactivity, acceptance, contemplation, apathy, and neutrality are quieter responses to common crises such as illness, loss of a loved one, retirement, or moving. Others react to stress differently through increased muscle tension or anxiety. The physical symptoms of stress are easier to alleviate when you know the cause. Again, talking with friends, keeping busy, taking up a new hobby, breathing exercises, and other group activities may help you enormously.

Independence depends on the number of choices you elect to make for yourself. Making plans, anticipating, and executing choices are keys to independent living. This does not mean that you need only to ponder choices in the large decisions. Daily living is composed of small ones as well. Some older adults focus on a new activity, such as bird watching, learning about antiques, or tutoring a child. It doesn't matter what it is as long as it interests you, takes your mind off yourself, and propels you toward personal control.

Those who have aged successfully have pride and a good self-image. They continue to feel and think young. They have the enthusiasm they had when young but now it has the added advantage of being tempered with the wisdom of their age. Serenity has replaced anxiety. They realize that with age they have become even more a unique person with a great deal to offer others because of their particular set of life experiences, beliefs, and insights.

Caregiving and Caretaking

One of the most common roles older people take on is caregiving. Spouses and adult daughters are the most common caregivers and contribute a huge amount of informal help to older adults in this country. People become caregivers for many reasons, most commonly because of their love, affection, commitment, and desire to reciprocate. Devotion to family members and not wanting to abandon a loved one are important motivators. Caregiving is an expression of the bonds that tie people to their loved ones and it allows caregivers to express intimacy, love, and other basic human emotions. This expression is needed to maintain continuity in values, self-respect, and identity. Caring and nurturing are important actions to maintain well being and purpose in life.

If you choose to live in a retirement community, you will

encounter some persons who need special modification of their environment, from dietary to remaining mobile. Sometimes people are suffering from some type of decrease in ability to remember that goes beyond the loss of explicit memory. Sensitive tolerance and the desire to understand others are needed to give social support to the individual and family. Not only will they appreciate and gain from these actions, but also the giver of such support will be rewarded through feelings of altruism, which bring increased self-awareness and mental health.

Although most people hate to think of the possibility, it may be that you yourself will become dependent on others for a short or longer time. After a lifetime of independence, you may find that you are no longer able to take care of yourself. Feeling vulnerable and unable to cope with the situation can put you in a situation that leads to depression. It is very important that you communicate your feelings and fears to a trusted family member, friend, or professional. If you find yourself in this situation, be realistic about your future.

If your dependence on others is for a short time only, such as need for physical care following an injury or illness, remember that it is for a limited period of time and try to regard this experience as one of added growth for yourself. Think back over all the times that you have been able to help others, and now ask for assistance when you need it from family and neighbors. Finding temporary and specific causes for misfortune is the art of hope.

However, not all reverses in health are temporary. Be realistic about your future and if you have to accept the fact that a return to your former functioning is not feasible, then make plans for your future based on your values and those who will be caring for you. Negotiate your role in decision making and communicate it to others. Make certain that your advance directives for health matters are up to date and that they clearly communicate your current wishes to your health providers and your family. Get all of your affairs in order, including legal documents.

Aging Gracefully

We can choose to age deliberately rather than accidentally. Take responsibility for your own aging. Seize the chance to grow older on your own terms. Become aware of your choices and plan for them while you are healthy. Relearn the optimism that is characteristic of youth. This requires "rewiring" your brain for thinking in new and more positive ways. It is important to realize that creativity does not necessarily decline as we grow older. As long as you remain healthy, both physically and emotionally, you will not experience a decline in your creative abilities. If you have been creative all your life, you are most likely to remain so now that you are older. In fact, with time for special projects you may even find that you have a spurt of creativity that you didn't know you had.

The abilities and opportunities of people living a long life carry new responsibilities. The traditional image of older age was one of withdrawal and disengagement. Older adults do not want to be dependent on others, but more importantly, those who are enjoying the gift of healthy aging feel they have much to offer younger generations. Older adults can use their experience and enduring energy to make significant contributions to the world. May you continue to find fulfillment as you age!

Resilience Test

The following questions are answered using a 5-point rating scale. If you strongly disagree with a statement, circle "1". If you are neutral about the statement, circle "3", and if you somewhat agree, circle "4".

	DISAGREE			AGREE	
1. I usually manage one way or another.	1	2	3	4	5
2. Keeping interested in things is important to me.	1	2	3	4	5
3. I feel proud that I have accomplished things in my life.	1	2	3	4	5
4. I usually take things in stride.	1	2	3	4	5
5. I am friends with myself.	1	2	3	4	5
6. I feel I can handle many things at a time.	1	2	3	4	5
7. I am determined.	1	2	3	4	5
8. I can get through difficult times because I have experienced difficulty before.	1	2	3	4	5

	DISAGREE			AGREE	
9. Self-discipline is important.	1	2	3	4	5
10. I keep interested in things.	1	2	3	4	5
11. I can usually find something to laugh at.	1	2	3	4	5
12. My belief in myself gets me through hard times.	1	2	3	4	5
13. In an emergency, I am someone people can generally rely on.	1	2	3	4	5
14. I can usually look at a situation in a number of ways.	1	2	3	4	5
15. My life has meaning.	1	2	3	4	5
16. When I am in a difficult situation, I can usually find my way out of it.	1	2	3	4	5
17. I am resilient.	1	2	3	4	5

Add the numbers that you have circled for your total Resilience score.

If your score is above 68, you are a resilient person and are likely to be flexible and adaptable when faced with a new situation. You have probably faced many challenges in your life and are able to keep a good perspective on the situation, knowing that you will get through.

If your score is below 68, you are less resilient, and may find that new situations or changes are very stressful for you. It may be helpful for you to consider how to mobilize the support you may need to get through the transition of moving. The help of family, friends and professionals can go a long way to ease your transition and help you re-establish balance in your life.

Financial Worksheet

This worksheet will help you compare your current costs with anticipated costs in each retirement community you tour. Fill in your current expenses in the left column and the costs you expect in the retirement community in the right column. Some costs may be included in the retirement community's monthly rental fee. Mark an "X" in the right column if the item is included in the monthly rental fee.

My Current Expenses

Expenses for a
Retirement Community

$ _____Rent or mortgage $ _____

$ _____Property taxes $ _____

$ _____Home or rental insurance $ _____

$ _____Utilities $ _____
          (Heat, sewer, water,
          garbage, electricity)

$ _____Food $ _____

$ _____Transportation $ _____

$ _____Parking $ _____

My Current Expenses

Expenses for a
Retirement Community

$ _____Car insurance

$ _____

$ _____Home maintenance/
yard work costs

$ _____

$ _____Laundry costs

$ _____

$ _____Entertainment

$ _____

$ _____Health care

$ _____

$ _____Other expenses

$ _____

$ _____TOTAL

$ _____

Clarifying Your Needs and Values

Place a check next to the items that you think you desire or may need now or in the future.

____ Assistance with household chores, laundry and yard work.

____ Assistance with shopping or meal preparation.

____ Assistance with daily living, such as bathing or dressing.

____ Access to nutritious meals.

____ Social support or companionship.

____ Recreational activities.

____ Educational opportunities.

____ Safety and security, with someone available to help if needed.

____ Health care consultation and assistance with health problems.

____ Rides to and from social activities, health appointments or shopping.

_____ Relief from or assistance with caring for a friend or family member.

_____ Training or equipment to help in coping with disabilities.

_____ Help with managing finances or seeking financial assistance.

_____ Help with legal matters.

Place a check next to the statements that summarize your views of the present and future:

_____ I have help available, but prefer not asking family or friends to help, or have difficulty getting needed assistance in my home.

_____ I will need help over a long period of time.

_____ I am willing to move from my present home.

_____ I am interested in living with other older people.

If you answered "yes" to any of the above four items, you may want to consider moving to a retirement community.

Shopping for Retirement Communities

As you shop for retirement communities, keep in mind what you are looking for, the types of needs/desires you have identified, your financial status and what each facility offers. The following questions may help you assess your options.

1) What is your general impression of the community? (Consider cleanliness, activity level, characteristics of residents and staff.)

2) Does the community offer the services and programs that you are seeking? (Check the menu, activity calendar and description of programs.)

3) What are the financial arrangements of the community? (Do they accept long-term care insurance, public assistance, is there a buy-in premium or a monthly rental fee?)

4) What is included in the monthly fees, for example, meals, personal care assistance, transportation, activities, utilities, etc.?

5) What are the admission and discharge criteria? Under what circumstances would a resident have to move from the community?

6) Are additional programs available if one's care needs change?

Other Helpful Resources

Bowman, F. J. (1989). *The Complete Retirement Handbook.* Lexington: University Press of Kentucky.

This book describes where you might want to move if you are interested in relocating after your retirement. It describes the cost of living in various parts of the country and talks about housing from the standpoint of geographical location.

Bridges, W. (1980). *Transitions: Making Sense of Life's Changes.* New York: Addison-Wesley.

How to cope with the difficult, painful and confusing times of change in your life. Outlines the phases of major transitions. This book has as its objective ways to handle these experiences as well as new insights that can help you learn about yourself.

The Consumer's Directory to Continuing Care Retirement Communities. (1993). American Association of Homes for the Aging, 901 E. Street NW, Suite 500, Washington, DC 20004-2037.

Contains facts and figures on continuing care retirement communities nationwide with a community profile by state. The profile includes a description of the setting, style of the community, sponsor and fee information. Probably the most complete directory of CCRCs on the market.

Cort, P., Ardsdale, V., & Newman, P. (1991). *Woman's Guide to Successful Retirement*. New York: Harper, Collins.
Limited to geographical location for housing.

Dychtwald, K., & Flower, J. (1989). *Age Wave*. Los Angeles: Tarcher.
An interesting book describing the changes taking place in society with the shift from youth orientation to increased life expectancy.

Friedman, J. P., & Harris, J. C. (1991). *Keys to Buying a Retirement Home*. New York: Barrons.
A real estate guide containing advice on financing, buying, assessing pros and cons of condos, planning maintenance, etc., on home buying for retirement living.

Kaufman, S. (1986). *The Ageless Self*. Madison, WI: University of Wisconsin Press.
Exploration of the attitudes, feelings and problems of later life including relationships, meaning, identity and personal reflection as perceived by some Americans age 70 to 97.

Lustbader, W. (1991). *Counting on Kindness*. New York: The Free Press.
A guide for caregiving families, both caregivers and receivers. Gives strategies for managing the emotional issues of dependency.

Matthews, J. (1993). *Beat the Nursing Home Trap*. Berkeley: Nolo Press.
Devoted to choosing and financing long-term care and describes organized elder residences. Discusses how to find congregate residences and protect assets.

Nelson, M. E., with Wernick, S. (2000). *Strong Women Stay Young.* New York: Bantam Books.

A motivating and informational book about exercise and the value of a strength-training program for women at any age. Gives easy to follow exercises that can be done at home in just two thirty minute sessions per week with ankle and wrist weights.

Perls, T. J., and Silver, M. H. (1999). *Living to 100: Lessons in Living to Your Maximum Potential at Any Age.* New York: Basic Books.

After studying more than one hundred centenarians the authors identify lifestyle patterns of those who age well. This book is filled with personal profiles, information, and a Life Expectancy Calculator.

Rowe, J. W., and Kahn, R. L., (1998). *Successful Aging.* New York: Pantheon Books.

Based on an extensive decade long study of aging sponsored by the MacArthur Foundation, this book describes how individual lifestyle choices determine how one ages.

Savageau, D. (1990). *Retirement Places Rated.* New York: Prentice Hall.

One hundred fifty-one retirement areas ranked and compared for cost of living, housing, climate, personal safety, services and leisure activities.

Seligman, M. (1990). *Learned Optimism.* New York: Pocket Books.

This book can help you change your mind and your life by learning to be optimistic about how you view your life.

Somers, A. R., & Spears, N. L. (1992). *The Continuing Care Retirement Community*. New York: Springer.

Written for health professionals and policy planners, this book has a helpful appendix reproduced from the American Association of Homes for the Aging guide for consumers. Contains the advantages and disadvantages in deciding if a particular community will meet needs, and describes a checklist that is helpful.